Creative Consciousness

The Unwritten Commandment

Volume 1

Creative Consciousness

The Unwritten Commandment

Volume 1

An angellic channeling through
Curt H. von Dornheim

™

ISBN 0-89404-220-3

Library of Congress Catalog Card No. 96-79384

Printed in the United States of America

Publisher:
AZTEX Corporation
P O Box 50046, Tucson, AZ 85703-1046

Creative Consciousness

What is Creative Consciousness? Is it a cause; is it a mission; is it a teaching; is it a way of life?

Creative Consciousness is the study and demonstration of Infinite, Intelligent, Creative Love through free will and co-creation resulting in the progression of kindness, compassion, honesty, justice, respect and equality for all souls upon Earth-Eden personally and collectively now and even after the change called death; hopefully ending the cycle of reincarnation permitting soulful progression to higher realms.

This message was received from a band of angels known as the Teaching Angels of Creative Consciousness through inspirational writing and speaking while in a channeling state of consciousness. It is scientific, philosophical and spiritual in that it investigates, explains and answers ontological questions pertaining to the existence of being through psychology, metaphysics and parapsychology.

The purpose of Creative Consciousness is to bring peace and enlightenment of higher standards upon Earth-Eden as rapidly as humanly and spiritually possible through these thirty chapters of progression. It is a spiritual aid and guide for persons of all religions and for persons of no religious affiliation.

Introduction

I heard: "The words shall be given unto you; therefore, write them down." I obeyed, and over a four year period, through the parapsychology of inspirational writing and speaking, wrote this textbook of metaphysics dealing with reincarnation, soul-progression and Creative Consciousness. I meditated and asked questions, then after a few short breathing exercises, having cleared my mind, I would go into an enlightened state of consciousness and listen to the angels. I heard and felt the words a split-second before I wrote. At first the words came with great speed, so much so that it was almost impossible to write them down. This is often called automatic-writing, trance-writing. I prefer to call it inspirational writing.

As I progressed, I was able to record on tape as I spoke slowly in an enlightened state of consciousness; this I call inspirational speaking. There are many names for this process such as sleep-talking, self-hypnosis, trance or channeling. People with this ability are often referred to as psychics, mystics, seers, mediums, sensitives or channelers. For some this may even be considered an out of the body experience. This is not new; rather, it has been a part of human existence for ages.

In the New Testament Paul mentions the difficulty at times of trying to distinguish between trance, dreams and out of the body experiences when he wrote: "It is not expedient for me doubtless to glory. I will come to visions and revelations of the Lord. I knew a man, whether out of the body I cannot tell, God knows; such as one caught up to the third heaven. And I knew a man whether in the body or out of the body I cannot tell. God knows." (2 Cor. 12:2-3). I feel that everyone has this ability in varying degrees, and if it is pursued honestly and patiently, progress can be made to this point of concentration.

Each chapter took from two to six meditative sessions and should be read with the understanding that it is more a verbal extemporaneous lecture than written word. It was received as one would take notes at a lecture, rather than as when one writes a literary work. When reading these pages, try to feel as if you are being taught by a group of wise and loving angel teachers who often re-emphasize various topics throughout, as these, my angelic co-authors, saw fit to repeat. I felt the book began with Chapter 5, and wanted to drop the first four chapters, but was instructed not to do so.

The book uses no gender pronouns except when mentioning certain known humans. It does not refer to God as "He" or "Father" but rather as "Infinite, Intelligent, Creative Love."

After the eighth chapter it was noticed that the last word of each chapter was also the subject title of the next.

I personally feel that these writings are old eternal wisdom taught in a new and provoking manner, thus shedding enlightenment on a new age in an old world.

My own words are this type face. **The words of my angel teachers are printed in this type face.** I truly believe the source to be Infinite, Intelligent, Creative Love *(the only source)*, which was then channeled through various souls in higher realms on to me. I also believe that the only purpose for human life on earth is for soul progression through kindness, compassion, honesty, justice, respect and equality, eventually enabling all souls to return home to our Creator.

Your channeling author upon Earth-Eden
Curt H. von Dornheim

Note: Many of the scripture verses are metaphysic interpretations

Preface

Earth, Earth, can you hear us? Earth-Eden, you upon the First Realm, listen to us, your loving teaching angels from the Third Realm. We can communicate! We are alive! We can help you. We are more alive now than when some of us were in the flesh.

Imagine where you would be today if the sciences were not permitted to progress, and only books written thousands of years ago were to be your sources of reference, as is unfortunately the case with many religions?

We are delighted to channel this book from the Third Realm where we dwell, through our dedicated colleague and instrument and your faithful mentor Curt, who dwells upon Earth-Eden, as we send this information on to him while he is in an enlightened state of consciousness. We wish to tell you that there *is* life after the change called death, and through this book hope to correct many wrong ideas, thus setting the record straight.

Don't you know you upon Earth-Eden *are* being watched? Don't you know your planet *is* in danger? Don't you wish to elevate your present standards of existence to those of a planet worthy of its relationship with the rest of the cosmos?

All of your days are numbered right up to your last breath! Predestination? Yes and no. A contradiction? No! A paradox? Yes! Every soul has made a commitment before having entered upon Earth-Eden in each reincarnation.

We hope that this book will lead you upon the path of progression. No one can travel well spiritually or physically without a path. A path is the way which has been traveled by those who follow others, having trust in the one who created that way originally. "And a little child shall lead them," the scriptures say, a soul without prejudice, a soul of innocence.

"Creative" means having the ability to bring into being that which evolves from a person's thinking. "Consciousness" means that part of you which is constantly aware (through the brain) of that to which the mind (the will of the soul) relates, thus resulting in Creative Consciousness. This is the understanding of the Love, the Creative, the Infinite, the Intelligent, the God within each one of you.

In order to gain enlightenment along this path of soul progression, study this textbook one page at a time, beginning with the first page, until you have reached the last. Mark, take notes, go back to re-read, but *do not* skip-read ahead. This is soulfully suggested for your progression. Only after you have read it once in this manner should you feel free to browse through it.

We say unto you, Curt, our channeling instrument of peace and enlightenment, as with the words of encouragement which Paul wrote in his letter to his dear friend Timothy: "Remain faithful to what you have learned and believe, knowing from whom you learned it. Preach the word, stay with the task whether convenient or not; correcting, repairing, appealing, constantly teaching and never losing patience." (2 Tim. 3:14 & 4:2)

You are guided, you are protected, you are loved.
Your angel teachers from the Third Realm

Dedication

The tenets of these chapters of progression
are dedicated personally to each and every one of you
who are sincere seekers of soul progression.

Your angel teachers from the Third Realm

Table of Contents

The Chapters of Progression

Chapter 1
Personal Progression

Anything which is a hindrance to your personal progression is inferior to you and can create a complex situation. Therefore, the term "inferiority complex" is not to be feared, but rather understood to be a situation which you will now begin to outgrow.

Make a study of the reasons for your personal complexes. As you find various sentences herein which apply to your personal problems, underline them and work with them on a daily basis, then note and watch your growth as the newly generated mental energies attract positive situations rather than negative ones.

Regardless whether the negative complexes resulted from early childhood or many years later, you do have the birth-given ability to rise above each and every one of these perceived problems *now*. Do not give any mental strength to the negative past, and concentrate not only on the positive future, but actually trust in Creative Love's concern for you *now*! It is by small yet constant steps that you ascend the staircase of personal progression, thus elevating your way of thinking, elevating your way of speaking, elevating your way of actually attracting situations which are of a higher standard—for like attracts like.

Words such as resurrection, reincarnation, salvation, assumption, ascension, victory and triumph have been used throughout the ages by various writers of numerous sacred books of the religions of the world. They were used in both physical and spiritual terms to express specific ideas and teachings. In a way, they all have a root meaning which is to rise above or to elevate, and that is precisely what you are beginning to do now. Once you think more highly of yourself, realizing that you are a reflection of Creative Love, you elevate your spirit, thus rising above your past through using mental positive energy from within. As you rise above mental doubts and negative images of yourself, you will find a new perception of the world from a higher viewpoint and begin to realize your endless possibilities of growth. You can be a strong person, a happy person, a calm person, a person who is progressing. You are a human being with the potential to become everything that is beautiful and good. With the constantly unfolding grand ability within yourself (which is your inalienable birth-right), this is possible.

Give no mental strength to false or negative ideas, rather turn your energy toward becoming the person whom you wish to be. Visualize yourself as the person whom you wish to be. Visualize yourself as the person whom you know you will become, and understand the simple principle that as you think, so you are, for you have free will.

Now we shall give you some Daily Lesson Sentences. Write them on separate small cards, keeping them with you for daily personal progression. Keep one at the place of your employment, in your handbag or wallet, or on the night table next to your bed. Read them aloud when possible, hearing your own encouraging voice once each hour of the day, then go to work silently and progress mentally. When you stumble on this upward path, remember that greater and lesser persons have done the same; *all* have stumbled, even Moses, Jesus, Lincoln and yourself. *All* who have tried have progressed. Later you will find that stumble-thoughts become less frequent, and eventually lose their pain as your trust in Creative Love grows.

DAILY LESSON SENTENCES

I have the mental strength of the universe within me.

I have complete power to overcome every needless anxiety.

Those who hesitate are not necessarily lost.

It is in the opposition that I receive during conquest from which I release the strength within me.

May my sadness always have the weight to push my lips downward in the middle to create a smile.

The greatest failure is to stop trying not to fail.

Progress is not always a grand step forward; sometimes it is a humble step to the side.

I shall not mortgage my future by discrediting someone else's past, for the mortgage rates for such an unwise investment are exceedingly high!

I shall not mistake selfish desires for goals.

Selfish desires can instill regressions deep within me; therefore I shall be careful as to the motives of my emotions.

To err is human, to forgive is also human and the beginning of soul progression.

I shall be still, and know that I am important. I shall be still and I shall know.

My spiritual reach should always exceed my physical grasp.

I shall become the master of myself rather than a slave, by sowing the seeds of progressive thoughts, which sprout into progressive words, which grow into progressive deeds, and which eventually reap a progressive destiny.

I shall not let the milk of human kindness sour with old age.

Passion, be it good or bad, tends to die in time if it is left to do so.

I shall strive to master simplicity in mental freedom and gain harmony with the universe.

Too often in the light of day, I make my own darkness. Too seldom in the dark of night, I remember that the light shall return in the morning. I shall strive for the light.

I shall strive to build a soul-progressive future. I shall build to be able to progress soulfully forever.

Daily I progress, in spiritual abundance.

Creative Love is the source which meets all my needs.

I shall care about myself as I care about others.

I shall check my thoughts constantly, to be progressive.

I have nothing to fear, for I trust in Creative Love's harmony with all people.

It is by small yet constant steps that I ascend the staircase of personal progression.

Pray the 23rd Psalm in the following manner with these enlightened concepts:
"Infinite, Intelligent, Creative Love is my Shepherd;
I shall not want, for Creative Love is the constant supply for all my needs both spiritual and physical.
This assurance lets me rest as in green pastures.
This supply constantly restores my soul's spiritual strength.
This Love leads me in righteous paths for Love's sake.
Yea, though I walk through the valley of the shadow of doubt, or death, I will fear no evil, for Love is constantly with

me, guiding me step by step.
Love's justice and Love's staff of support, they comfort and protect me.
Love has prepared a table of spiritual and physical abundance before me in the presence of my enemies, who do not follow Love's Ways.
Love anoints my head with the oil of healing ideas, my cup of life overflows.
Goodness and mercy shall follow me all the days of my present incarnation, and I shall progress to dwell in Love's ways forever."

In order to achieve personal progression, you must change your concepts of all past thoughts which have not brought you personal progression. *Change your concepts!* You have the power available to change non-progressive concepts into personal progression. Remember, it is by small yet constant steps that you ascend the staircase of personal progression.

One sure way to change your concepts into personal progression is to constantly *replace* each and every negative thought with the new concept of how Creative Love wishes you to be. After having done this on a daily basis for perhaps a week, you will begin to notice not only a gradual personal progression, but also a profound inner peacefulness.

Take weekly stock of your personal progression. Write down two or three concepts which you wish to change about yourself. At the end of the week, go over the list and evaluate your progress. Do not be disappointed if you have not progressed as quickly as you had wished, for that too is personal progression in that you *want* to progress quickly. But remember, it is by small yet constant steps that you ascend the staircase of personal progression.

Continue to use the Daily Lesson Sentence Cards. However after about three weeks begin to pick out key words from the cards, using them as Mini-Concept-Changers. Then begin to include them in your daily meditation. You will be surprised how quickly you can cast out negative thoughts by using this method. For example, if a doubt creeps in concerning your entrance into a room filled with strangers, and you have been working with overcoming fear of strangers, you need only to think of the words "Creative Love's harmony" to bring confidence from the Daily Lesson Sentence which says, "I have nothing to fear, for I trust in Creative Love's harmony with all people," or, from our transcription of the 23rd Psalm, think of the word "constantly" which says, "Yea, though I walk through the valley of the shadow of doubt or death, I will fear no evil, for Love is *constantly* with me, guiding me step by step."

One of the most seemingly difficult concepts to change is the separation or loss of a loved one. Although this may seem difficult, such concepts *can* be overcome with these same methods. But like all concepts, you must accept the loss, then *want* to change the concept of the loss. Hurting can fade away, and love can grow if given the opportunity. The pain of death does not last, but love does span the gulf of the grave.

Here is a short poem in which the word "phantom" tells of the nothingness of self-pity and where the last sentence states a fact of existence.

BE STILL

Be still, O phantoms of the heart,
Show not your shadows deep within.
Wear a countenance freshly washed,
So none will know your woeful pain.

Be still, O phantoms of the heart,
Enwrap your loss not as a cloak.
In hurt lie also balms of healing,
And strength to give you greater love.

Be still, O phantoms of the heart,
Body and soul you still possess.

Keep on the path which seeks the morrow,
Since you journey not alone.

You journey not alone, *not alone*! *All* human beings are in the state of human life together, and *all* can be one with each other and one with Infinite Intelligence and the universe. *All* have hurts, *all* can overcome and learn to change these concepts to gain personal progression by trusting in Creative Love.

For all the yesterdays which have passed and cannot return, for all the tomorrows which have not yet arrived with their great expectations, there is the ever-present in which you can progress with the wisdom of the past and the hope for the future, through trust in Creative Love which dwells within you. This is "Yestermorrow!"

Remember that positive thoughts create more positive thoughts. Look at others in a positive way and you will soon realize that positiveness reflects positiveness. Learn to trust others as a step in the staircase of personal progression, even though such trust may seem like a risk at the time; remember that "nothing ventured, nothing gained" is a truism. Trust in the future, have no reluctant ideas about it, for that future has never come in one large lump. It always has and always will come just one day at a time, one hour at a time, one minute at a time, one second at a time. You have been able to manage so far, but now you will progress with the help of Creative Love in which you are learning to trust.

Learn to listen to Infinite Intelligence, to your inner self, and to others. As you listen more to Infinite Intelligence, you will begin to understand it more. As you listen more to yourself, you will begin to understand yourself more. As you listen more to others, you will begin to understand others more; thus you will begin to understand life more. Believe in yourself, and in your motivations. Exercise the universal, creative power within yourself. Decide to prosper through personal progression, and believe that you can! Creative, Loving, Infinite Intelligence has given that power to you. Associate with positive people who have positive ideas, then become mentally and

1 physically productive, by being more meditative.

Chapter 2
Meditative Progression

A necessity on the path of progression is meditation. Meditation is thought, and to borrow from an old phrase, "grow in thought, word and deed."

Look at the first word of this trio, "thought." A good method for progression of thought is through meditation. Each person must find the method best suited to individual needs.

One of the simplest and easiest ways which we suggest for meditating alone or within a group is as follows: first, silently speak to yourself, then listen to your inner self. Have the room dimly lit, at a moderate temperature, with the windows covered to the outside. Be seated in a comfortable chair, yet not so comfortable as to cause sleep to occur. If alone, meditate upon the following "suggestion journey," or if in a group, (after a silent prayer of protection) have the leader speak the following in a slow, soft voice:

"Close your eyes, take a few very deep, long breaths and begin to relax. Feel your toes and feet slowly relaxing, feel your legs and thighs relaxing, feel your abdomen, arms, hands and fingers relaxing, then finally feel your shoulders, throat and head relaxing pleasantly and completely.

"Now, envision in your mind's eye that you are at a gathering in a beautiful meadow filled with lovely flowers. A pleasant breeze blows through the high shade trees in the distance, and you feel the breeze gently flowing through your hair, mingling with the soothing warmth of the overhead sun. You meet a group of interesting, progression seeking people. Although there may be no one whom you know in the group, there is a feeling of familiarity and closeness among all of you.

"A friendly guide begins to lead the group on a journey. Its path leads slowly to the right at the edge of the meadow among the trees beside a fresh-running brook which rushes joyously along its way. The guide stops momentarily for a cool drink and several of the group do the same. The water is refreshingly pure. After a short rest you continue along the forest path following the brook toward its source. There the trees become more sparse, and you begin to see beautiful blooming bushes which release a delightful fragrance into the clean country air.

"As you progress onward, the guide leads the group into a clearing and in the distance the path begins to incline. Slowly the way becomes a bit steeper, yet easy to tread. Not too far away the light green ivy grows up along the rock which rises to form the mountain ahead. You keep climbing until a small plateau is reached where there are several benches carved in the granite by the hands of time. Wild roses ramble along natural arbors, and mingle with the ivy. Your guide invites all of you to be seated and rest while awaiting your individual turn to privately ascend farther for one of the most memorable moments of your life.

"As you quietly sit and wait, you can hear the brook from farther up as it cascades downward in a small waterfall, and the music of many lovely song-birds. There is a quiet, calm trust encompassing you as your thoughts drift in such serenity. Soon your guide approaches and asks you to follow. Together you walk slowly a bit farther up the path, under a rainbow which spans a bridge over the waterfall. Then comes into view a strong, overhanging cliff-roof which is the entrance to a sunlit grotto in the side of the mountain. Before it, you see standing bathed in the sun's array, an ancient, caring and wise-looking soul.

"Your guide tells you that you may ask this concerned angel for the answer to any question which is of most importance to you at this point in your life, and that you *will* receive a true and honest answer.

"Your guide steps aside as you climb alone the remaining few well-worn steps with assuredness and trust. You enter the sunlit grotto and the benevolent angel bids you to be seated in one of two seats. The angel takes the other seat and with a compassion-filled countenance asks you to state your question or situation. You speak slowly, presenting your request. You pause for a moment and then listen in earnest as your angel advises you."

After a period of at least three minutes, the leader of the group says in a slow and positive voice: "Our journey has ended. One: you feel relaxed. Two: you feel strengthened. Three: you feel refreshed. Four: you feel peaceful. Five: you will now open your eyes."

When everyone's eyes have become accustomed to the room again, the leader asks all to write down their questions and the answers received. They may remain private if the individual prefers it so, or may be discussed at this time. All notes should be kept for further reference and comparison after several of these mental journeys. It is suggested that there be only one session per week—at the same time—on the same day—in the same place, in order to create a familiar pattern, and to open and close each session with silence. As you study your questions and answers over a period of six weeks, you will begin to realize the speed of your growth through meditation. You may eventually take journeys to wherever you wish. However, be careful of your motives!!

The second word in the trio is "word." It is natural to talk about an idea before it becomes a reality. Group discussion is valuable but occasionally, private counseling may still be necessary. Those who cannot yet share in open discussion can benefit as listeners; however, as time goes on, they should be encouraged to become part of the discussion.

Group discussion is necessary and should be listened to by the speaker as well as by the others. Insincere ramblings are of no value, can cause disruption rather than growth, and therefore should be treated as something to be overcome. Only in extreme instances should anyone be asked to leave the group, and even then should be given a sincere invitation to rejoin after further personal progression. In no way is authority to be abused.

The last word in the trio is "deed." "Deed" should always have the word "good" as its adjective. The one important thing to remember about a deed is that once it is done, it cannot be undone! If it is a regressive deed, the best it can be elevated to is a non-progressive deed by one's trying to counteract it. Therefore, it is with wisdom of the past that one should plan a deed in order to bring about progression, which then leads to hope for the future.

Past deeds are of great value in discussion groups. Much can be learned by yourself and others from your own deeds and the deeds of others. Always remember to keep kindness in mind when in group discussion. Everyone is of utmost importance, no matter how far a person may have regressed. Demonstrating kindly concern for friend or stranger is a sure way to stop regression. There is *never* a point of no return.

What are you? Who are you? You are the highest form of intelligent life upon Earth-Eden with ability to meditate. You are souls of hope with every possibility under the sun to help others to meditate through your intrinsic union with each other and with Infinite Intelligent universal harmony. You can accomplish endless progression through meditating upon kindness. Preference is given to the word "kindness" rather than the word "love" simply because the word "love" has been so greatly abused. "Love" has been dragged down to mean anything from lustful sexual acts to plain ordinary greed. Thank goodness the word "kindness" seems still to have kept its meaning.

To use the word "Love" for one moment in the fullest extent of its meaning, let us say this to you: You are Love, and that Love is the creative motivation of the entire universe. Love is the core of life, and unfortunately too often many do not live up to the grand virtues in life of which all are capable. Remember you have the power to progress personally, to help others to progress personally, and to evolve in unity through Creative Love in the universe. All of this is part of meditation: to muse, to ponder, to consider abstractly. During the day be aware of various thoughts, words and deeds which are not for your progression. You can change these into progression by replacing them with constructive concepts, as you slowly yet constantly ascend the staircase of meditative progression!

Meditation can also be practiced in the following ways:

Sitting beside a warm fireplace and watching the flickering flames may bring to mind the pangs of needless pain suffered in the past, and how, with time, the pangs slowly either soared higher with the fuel of emotion, or burned out.

Sitting in the desert and wrestling with your innermost temptations may bring to mind the Master Teacher Jesus' victory over the same temptations through the strength which is found planted deeply within.

Sitting on a high mountain and watching the billowing clouds go by may bring to mind the majestic ideals and plans which you expect to fulfill in this space of time allotted in this incarnation.

Sitting beside the sea and watching the waves roll in may bring to mind the eons of time during which Earth-Eden existed before you entered upon it, and the eons of time during which it will continue to exist after you have left it to progress beyond the ebb tides of this life.

Through prayerful meditation one can begin to understand intuitively with the heart what the brain often does not understand. This is the way through which to open the channel for Creative Consciousness to enter into one's mind, one's words and one's actions, thus bringing about much opportunity for soul progression.

Take these very valuable lessons of life and set them aside to meditate upon. Feel the strength of the wisdom within you, responding to Infinite Intelligence, from whence comes constant counseling.

Chapter 3
Counseling Progression

A problem shared is a problem half-solved because it is the admitting of one's needs. *All* need Creative Love and each other to help solve their problems, and any who think differently are grossly in error.

Human beings are the most highly developed creatures upon Earth-Eden, with the ability to constantly use the mental tools of progression. Some of these tools are: kindness, compassion, honesty, justice, respect, equality, empathy, hope, wisdom, joy and trust, as well as many other rewarding abilities. It is with these that the loving mentor is to give counsel. There is a vast difference between counselor and mentor; to be a counselor alone is not enough—one must also be a mentor!

A counselor is one who gives interchange of opinion, advice or consultation deliberate in purpose or design. A mentor is much more than that. A mentor *must* care. A mentor *must* be a friend, advisor, teacher, counselor and guide who is wise enough to forgive wrong-doings without being a judge or confessor. A mentor *must* help the seeker to trust in Infinite Intelligence, and also to help the seeker to follow the mentor's wise instructions. This is not the role for everyone, yet there could be many more mentors than there are; many are called, but *few* have chosen to help.

Being a mentor also means following Love's ways by putting aside false ego, false pride and selfishness. This calls for the highest compassion toward the lowest, a positive personality toward the negative, and a sense of humor where there is none. A mentor never condemns the seeker, only the non-progressive concept, always following Love's ways.

It is quite natural to be attracted more to some people than others for spiritual, physical, intellectual and reincarnative reasons; therefore, choose your mentor with care. Mentors vary as greatly as do seekers, and for each plaint of a seeker, there is the guidance of a mentor. No matter how deep or great is your plaint, there is a wiser and compassionate mentor, who as the needed balm of Gilead soothes you, helps you to listen to yourself, and teaches you to listen to that still small voice within. Once you have reached this point of meditation where you can ponder upon a given problem and find the answer from within, you will learn that it is *always truthful*! You may not always care for the answer, but Love's still, small voice within is always honest and truthful. It's up to each of you to obey that wisdom of the inner-mentor, or to reject it and pay the consequence.

One of the main points in counseling is to cultivate the garden of thoughts within you. Then work with that progression to help cultivate the garden of thoughts in others, by pulling out the weeds of non-progressive concepts and replacing them with seedlings of progressive concepts. Remember, it is by small yet constant steps that one helps others to ascend the staircase of progression, through common-sense-counseling and trust in Infinite Intelligence.

Never give advice which you yourself would not or could not follow. Never give advice to make yourself seem important or as the "great wise-one." Never give advice of a tenth-grade level to a second-grader. The best rules to follow are examples and past experiences of your own progression. Be flexible, always keeping in mind that each person is an individual who may not necessarily progress personally in the same manner or with the same speed as you; therefore, alterations in concepts, advice and methods may be necessary. Bring to mind once more the trio in the past chapter on meditation of "thought, word and deed." Remember that silent prayer and meditation are a must and a prelude to counseling. The mentor must be calm, compassionate and receptive. Silent prayer and meditation help set that mood.

Concept-changing is a prime method to be used by the wise mentor in counseling. The mentor must kindly point out to the seeker any non-progressive concepts, then understandingly help the seeker to replace them with progressive concepts.

As a mentor you can also counsel the seeker in other ways, such as by scripture parables, stories, poetry, history, or whatever may best suit the age and mental level of the seeker. In prose counseling there is much to be learned. Here is an example:

Be a leader to those whom you can teach,
yet a follower of those from whom you can learn.

Be poor in false pride,
yet rich in kindness.

Be empty of unrighteous judgment,
yet filled with patience.

This little prose-mentor can encourage the seeker to overcome regression of false pride and false judgment with progression in kindness and patience. It also encourages the seeker to rise to the mentor level, yet reminds the mentor of more highly progressed mentors.

Remember, counsel without kindness is not progressive. Kindness, however, does not always mean giving in; yet kindness is always just and strong, following the ways of Creative Love through the myriad forms of Infinite Intelligence, such as meditation, counseling and prose.

Chapter 4
Prose Progression

The eternal optimists are those who say when their cups are nearly empty, "Look! There is still some left!"

It is all well and good to keep in step with a distant drummer, as long as you don't throw anyone out of step who is in keeping with the local drummer.

Learn to relax as the cat, to rest as the cat, to be patient as the cat, to be independent as the cat; perhaps then there will be less anxiety, restlessness, frustration and fear.

One is happy when one has known what it was to have been unhappy.

"He (Infinite Intelligence) shall give his (Creative Love) angels orders to guard and watch over you closely and care fully (personally)" (Luke 4:10). Some of those angels are in human form!!

Let not false morality fool you with its misuse of the word love. Love is still benevolence, not self-indulgence.

Jealousy in life is like spice in a cake. A little bit often brings out a hidden savor; too much ruins it all.

Do not build your dream castle upon the stones of someone else's ruins.

Many times the heart accepts what the brain cannot comprehend.

Saying "I'll forgive, but I'll never forget" is the same as saying "I'll throw away the photo, but I'll keep the negative and, whenever I feel like it, I'll have reprints made."

To serve does not always mean to do what you are told. To serve often means to do what you must.

Tomorrow is the eternal traveler, always on its way.

The oldest wine is not necessarily the best.

The tiny seeds found inside a grape are vineyards which have not yet come to their fullest potential. It takes four ingredients to create a vineyard: labor, time, growth, and love.

There are many reasons for reaching the end of a road.

The costs of the greedy desires which you fulfill are paid in the price of hardships to others and yourself. The profits of the loving kindnesses which you fulfill are credits in the accounts of benevolence to others and yourself.

Just as the harp does not sound before it is plucked, so can there be no forgiveness before there is kindness. Just as thunder does not roar before lightning, so can there be no redemption before there is contrition.

As a stream endlessly seeks the sea, so you should endlessly try to seek kindness within yourself and others.

There is a time for all seasons to begin, and there is a time for all seasons to end.

What is death? What is birth? They are one and the same. It depends upon which life you are in at the time. Death is the birth into the next life, as birth is the dying from the life before.

A raindrop, with imagination, can become a sea. It is up to each of you to sink or swim in that sea, or that rain drop.

Dream to build a future. Build to dream forever.

At various times some look toward the rainbow, some look toward themselves, some look toward others, and in all is found Creative Love.

When you overburden or abuse your soul, it often wants to forget as much as to forgive.

Just as there cannot be a shadow without a light to cast it, so there cannot be a soul lost without Creative Love wanting its return.

As tears bring freedom, so trials bring growth.

Those who blow their own trumpets have already received their applause from their own fanfare.

Just as the sweet fragrance of the blossom is a continuation of its beauty, so is the hope of a youth's broken heart; for longing is a continuation of love.

All which exists is universally unified.

Strive to master simplicity in spiritual freedom and gain harmony with the universe.

Soar for the empyreal.

To whom much is given, much is expected.

How can you console those who crave that which you possess because of your life's progressions? Greed cannot be consoled, only exposed!

How fortunate are they who have someone to shed tears over, for it means that they love. How sad for those who do not have the circumstances to do so.

If one has studied and does not fulfill what one was taught in mind, word and action, then one has not learned, but has merely been confronted with that knowledge.

When life is easy, one often forgets the hardships.
And when life is difficult, one often remembers.
Often hardships teach one life's values.
And comforts rob one of life's values.

Many who wear the collar are often not reverend. Many who do not, are often ordained by a higher hand. By their deeds shall you know them!!!

One must leave the forest to think about it clearly.

'Tis a shame that the sound which speaks from the pipes of a majestic organ on Sunday morning is at times more rewarding than that of the sound from the pulpit!!!

Echoes and mirrors are cousins in the family of truth, for they both cannot lie.

Infinite Intelligence should be the center of religion, for it is the very center of existence.

A poem should not exceed the limits of its importance.

One person's wrong may be another's right, depending upon the justice of the situation.

Capacity of excellence can never be exceeded by dominance.

One of the dullest sounds known is an unenthusiastically spoken "Alleluia"!!!

Be careful when you think you are in love. Be sure you are in love with a person, and not in love with the cause of being in love.

Beware of fearful thoughts, for that which you fear may well come upon you. Are you gaining in strength of thought? Remember, thought is energy!

Beware of those who have it "all wrapped up!"

An Infinite, Intelligent, oriented soul is never lost or in the wrong place, for Infinite Intelligence is order.

There are many little valleys in each person's life through which they must pass. There are many little hills in each person's life which they must climb. Few of you scale Everest, but all of you enter into the valley of the shadow of death, and that's all it is, only a shadow; and in order to have a shadow, there must be a light to cast it!

If you never leave home you can never enjoy the experience of returning. If you never feel the pain of being wronged, you can never have the opportunity to feel the consolation of forgiveness. If you never stray from Creative Love, you can never experience the joy of reconciliation. Since you *have* strayed from Creative Love, we ask you, what are you doing to reconcile yourself?

It is strange that a lack of some essentials can create the same amount of regression as an overabundance. Not enough money can cause one to steal, and too much money can cause one to neglect others. Not having obtained love can cause hatred toward others, while being fortunate enough to have a love can cause one to forget about the feelings of those who are alone.

Have you ever seen a forsythia bush bring forth its blossoms at the *end* of the season in the bitter cold? You will find this in people. Compare this to an older person who becomes like a child. Have you ever seen a pear tree heavy laden with fruit in early spring *before* it has blossomed? You will find this in the likes of a child who is old for its age.

There was an old soul toiling heavily in the heat of the day, planting a vineyard. A passerby came and questioned, "Old one, what are you doing?" The old soul replied, "I am planting a vineyard." The passerby rebuked, "You are foolish, for at your age you will never live to the day when you can enjoy the fruits of your labors." The old soul smilingly replied, "But you see, I must do this because I am obligated, for others have planted vineyards before me so that I was able to drink of the vine; therefore, now I, in turn, plan to build a vineyard for those who will come after me so that they too may taste!" This is true caring.

Many are called but *few* have chosen to follow the calling in their hearts. Alas, what a loss! Do they know what a loss they have chosen to accept for themselves and others? Have you been called? Have you chosen to follow your calling? Remember the rich man whom the Master Teacher called to follow Him? The man chose not to do so. Imagine rejecting Jesus in person? Did the rich man know whom he had chosen to reject? Regardless of how large or how small the various callings may be, regardless of how young or how old you are, each individual calling is custom-made for the likes of *you*, and therefore each acceptance or rejection is custom made by the likes of *you*. Which shall it be? It is in *your* hands. Which shall it be?

CHRISTMAS

Follow the day-star of equality which shines forth, guiding the path of each seeking wise soul. There find the nativity of unadorned, foundational Truth in the cradle of simple, understanding Trust, guarded by sacred, virgin Love.

And there, leave your gifts of golden honesty, frankincense-like silent prayers of thanks rising above selfishness, and spiritual myrrh-wisdom for the anointing and preservation of the teachings of Creative Consciousness to be shared with friend and stranger for the progression of souls, thus becoming a watchful shepherd of compassion by doing the Will of Infinite, Intelligent, Creative Love.

NEW YEAR

Let it be as in years gone by that the hearts of you good-willed hearts upon Earth-Eden do again reflect upon the life which has been given to you from the Life.

Let it be as in years gone by that the minds of you good-willed minds upon Earth-Eden do again reflect upon the all which has been given to you from the All.

Let it be as in years gone by that the souls of you good-willed souls upon Earth-Eden do again reflect upon the existence which has been given to you from the Existence.

REALM of TRUST

She had what many did not. Her husband was a man of high rank. His ego told her ego of their physical beauty. Her garments were of the finest silks and satins sewn by the most gifted of hands. Her abode was furnished from lands beyond the seas. Her jewels a mighty ransom could bring. She bathed in the purest of oils and sunned in a spa of fame. Her offspring she gave the best of schooling, her friends were chosen with the care and strategy of a general. She loved her mate, her offspring, her friends and her life, and feared those things which wealth could not change such as disease, pain, forsakedness, loneliness, death and the unknown.

She had a servant who had little. Her husband was a lowly laborer. His ego told her ego of their physical plainliness. Her garments were of the coarsest of linen, sewn by the most tired of hands. Her abode was furnished from the local surroundings. Her jewels were beads of faded glass, which would ransom nothing. She washed in the water of the village well, and sunned in the fields while laboring. Her offspring she gave the same self-learning which she had experienced; her friends were chosen as a result of her daily tasks. She loved her mate, her offspring, her friends, and her life, and feared those things which poorness could not change such as disease, pain, forsakedness, loneliness, death and the unknown.

Although there were countless differences between the two women, the importance was in what each sought in her heart. Whether rich or poor, had either first sought more trust in Creative Love, her life's fears would have been eliminated beyond imagination, for fear is nothing more or less than lack of trust in Infinite, Intelligent, Creative Love.

Earth-Eden is not your goal in any way, shape or form. You need *not* return endlessly through reincarnation.

Chapter 5
Reincarnative Progression

We wish to mention at this point what seems to have been concepts concerning reincarnation in the past and what some people think about it in the present.

Reincarnation is accepted by many as the belief that the soul, upon the death of the body, is reborn into another body or form—a rebirth of the soul in successive bodies. Study groups, some organized religions and millions who have no religious affiliations consider this a fact rather than a religious idea. Even today many members of the Jewish and Christian faiths who do not teach reincarnation will admit their acceptance of it behind closed doors.

The Egyptians believed in a physical afterlife beneath Earth-Eden after death. Their symbols of the ankh and the scarab were constant reminders. Today millions still consider reincarnation a fact without putting any great religious stress upon it, simply accepting it!

There is the belief that a soul must grow through eons of time by beginning with the lowest forms of life and gradually working itself up to the higher forms with the final step being human.

Others say this is not the case, rather that each species is in a class of its own, and one could never be in the other group. Some say that reincarnation works for all species but not for humans.

Next is the idea that humans can reincarnate as other species. Some say no form can regress. It is quite a varied subject.

Then come numerous ideas about the reasons for reincarnation. Basically, many seem to agree with the idea that the main reason is for growth, or progression of life. Besides biological growth, some believe it is for psychological and spiritual growth. Then there are the ideas that there is a series of either religious, physical and/or cosmic laws which determine the reason for being reincarnated, or reaching the end of the reincarnative process. These laws are supposed to be based upon the type of existence which each individual species or human demonstrated in preceding incarnations. This, in the human form, is to be a type of judgment or evaluation of one's life, to be pronounced either by the individual (self meeting self,) by some higher soul or souls, by gods or God who will determine into what situation the soul shall be born in its next incarnation. The law has been given the name Karma (cause and effect).

So far we have been speaking only about the ideas of reincarnation as it is known in a three dimensional, physical existence on this planet. There are beliefs that there are reincarnations (or spiritual transformations) which are non-physical, occurring in other dimensions, on other planets in the universe, in which one type of reincarnation then progresses to another type of reincarnation in an evolutionistic process beyond what is called time and space in your present limited existence in a three-dimensional physical world.

You surely have read articles and heard stories of those who swear they feel that they can remember bits of past lives. The French call it *"déjà vu;"* which means, "having seen before." Many have gone to places where they have never been before and yet have had feelings of familiarity, even to the point of knowing what is around a corner. There are also certain types of dreams that make one feel very much at home; dreams of familiar yet unfamiliar places or people. These dreams are claimed to be remembrances of past incarnations.

Some have met strangers with whom they immediately felt comfortable. Some have met strangers with whom they immediately felt uncomfortable. It is believed by some that these individuals may have known each other in past incarnations and are recalling past feelings.

In the East there are recorded episodes where young children have gone into villages miles from their homes and have correctly identified members of the family of a deceased person whom the child claimed to have been. In the West there are some cases of age regression where it is claimed that people have given information of past lives which has been documented, researched and proven to be correct.

Age regression sessions are becoming frequent, with more persons wanting to understand their lives and their roots. All too often, some overstructured religions leave one with only the word "faith" and nothing more when it comes to confronting the change called death. Some teach that life after death is a promise by God, yet supply any proof of it and they call it the work of the devil.

Let us also remind you of the many psychics who have given hundreds of "readings" on reincarnation while in trance, and often after their deaths. Through the tedious task of cross-filing these readings, the claims of validity of the readings have grown.

There are some groups who believe in a set reincarnative time-period occurring every one hundred forty years, with a seventy-year life span here, and a seventy-year life span elsewhere. Elsewhere? Where elsewhere? Others believe you can reincarnate only after having finished a specific task which was chosen before birth to be accomplished, and that reincarnation can be either a punishment for self, or a choice to help others.

This is but a short yet basic outline of various concepts concerning reincarnation. Physical evidence on this subject is difficult to show because it cannot be easily researched, encompassing religious, cultural and personal concepts, as well as the passage of time.

Those accepting reincarnation, although their ideas differ, are somewhat united in one thought; for the most part they do not believe in missionizing the idea of reincarnation. They feel that the law of reincarnation, like the law of gravity, exists for everyone whether it is believed or not and that all will be reincarnated according to the way they have lived their lives.

Now we will explain reincarnation to you, beginning with the law of Karma!! Karma is the second greatest cosmic law, the law of cause and effect. This is the law which automatically goes into action when the first and preferred law of Grace is neglected or rejected! Karma is the main reason for reincarnation and can be overcome by Grace, thus ending the reincarnative cycle.

Why do you not remember all your past incarnations? To say it would be a distraction would be the understatement of the ages. If the past lives were good, it could cause conceit and create regression. If the past lives were far from good, it could cause discouragement and lack of confidence. Your conscious brain has forgotten much of the past in this present incarnation; for if you did remember everything, it would simply be too much clutter for the brain. Imagine what confusion would be in the brain if all past incarnations were constantly present. The mind of the soul, however, *does* remember and takes inventory between incarnations. A trained individual after much proper meditation can recall. Even without meditation, glimpses can be remembered if one knows what to look for. *Déjà* vu is but one example, that familiar feeling of a place which you have never visited in this present lifetime. Remembering is not generally of great importance on the Earth-Eden level. If it is truly needed for an individual, it will be made known.

Let us remind you of the numerous passages in the writings of the great religions of the world which mention and teach about reincarnation. Reincarnative references can be found in the Kabbalah, the Apocrypha, the Old Testament, the New Testament and in various other ancient scriptures. In the New and Old Testaments these teachings can still be found if you seek avidly enough. You must keep in mind, however, that through the last several thousand years there have been many rewritings of the Bible, and therefore there have been many deletions, additions and changes by so-called theologians, many of whom claim to be correct. Now we ask you, *how could all of them have been correct* when the Catholic and Protestant Bibles do not contain the same books, and even argue about which books are or are not so-called Holy Writ? Let us also remind you that the books which were chosen to become the Old and the New Testaments were chosen through vote by councils of humans. In the last fifty years alone there have been alterations made which change *many* meanings.

We wish to give to you, our seekers, a few passages containing examples which still mention reincarnation. For more information you can obtain reference books which are available on that subject.

"Whereupon are the foundations (of Earth-Eden) thereof fastened? Or who laid the cornerstone thereof? When the morning stars sang together, and all the sons (souls) of God (Creative Love) shouted for joy." (Job 38:6-7)

This quotation from the Old Testament has been used in poetry and hymnology for thousands of years. Notice that all souls were there when the stars were created. All certainly not in the physical, but most certainly in spirit. Not only is there life after death, but there is life before birth!!

"And when Jesus came into the courts of Caesarea Philippi, he asked his disciples, saying, 'Whom do men say that I the Son of man am?' And they said, 'Some say that Thou art John the Baptist; some, Elias, and others, Jeremiah, or one of the prophets.'" (Matt. 16:13-15)

How could they have thought Jesus to be one of those who had been dead for hundreds of years if not for a belief in reincarnation?

"And his disciples asked him (Jesus), saying, 'Why then say the scribes that Elias must first come?' And Jesus answered and said unto them, 'Elias truly shall first come, and restore all things. *But I say unto you, that Elias is come already, and they knew him not,* but have done unto him whatsoever they listed. Likewise shall also the Son of man suffer of them.' *Then the disciples understood that he spoke unto them of John the Baptist!*" (Matt. 17:10-13)

Here we see that Jesus told His own disciples that John was the reincarnation of Elias. It cannot be taken to mean anything else. Those theologians who cross this off as a likeness or parable still cannot explain away the part where Jesus tells that "likewise shall also the Son of man (Jesus) suffer." That also came to pass!

"And as Jesus passed by, he saw a man who was *blind from birth.* And his disciples asked him saying, 'Master, who did sin, this man, or his parents, that he was born blind?' Jesus answered, 'Neither has this man sinned, nor his parents: but that the works of God

(Creative Love) should be made manifest in him.'" (John 9:1-3) How could this man who was *blind from birth* have sinned? When? In the womb? Needless to say, the disciples *did* believe in the second highest law of Karma, in that he and his parents may have sinned in a past life, causing him to have been born blind in this incarnation. But, he could have *chosen* his soul to be reincarnated blind so that Creative Love could be made manifest in him through the Master's demonstration of Creative Consciousness, thus gaining soul progression from his loss of sight and ending his time under Karma by gaining Grace, therefore needing to reincarnate *no more*, needing to "go out *no more*" (Rev. 3:12).

Remember, Earth-Eden is not your goal, Heaven is! Not all suffering is punishment, just as not all learning is difficult, but much soul progression can be obtained by what seems to the unknowing as suffering.

"Him that overcometh (self, selfishness, greed; the root sin) will I make a pillar (strong) in the temple of my god (Infinite Intelligence), and he shall go out no more." (Rev. 3:12)

Go out to where? The soul upon perfecting itself through a number of reincarnations, leaves the power of the second highest law of Karma and does not need to go out into a physical body again, having reached the power of the highest law of Grace (Infinite Love).

"Behold I (Jesus) stand at the door and knock: If anyone hears My voice, and opens the door, I will come to them, and will sup with them, and they with me. To those that overcometh I will grant to sit with me on my throne, *even as I also overcame* and am set down with my Father in His throne (Infinite, Intelligent, Creative Love). Those that have ears, let them hear what the Spirit says to the churches." (Rev. 3:20-22)

Here we find that even the Galilean Pathshower had to overcome "self" in order to achieve Grace. A dire message to the churches from the Spirit of Holiness!!

The soul of the Master has entered upon Earth-Eden many times at various intervals. The last time was nearly two thousand years ago. This was the most dramatic, most humble, most enlightened reincarnation of that redeeming soul known as the Christ, who has been the Pathshower upon Earth-Eden for thousands of years.

The reason that the last incarnation was so powerful, having such a tremendous effect on billions of entities upon Earth-Eden and lasting for twenty centuries, is because the Master's soul entered in dual form; that is to say, with its soul mate, or other half known as the entity Mary. It also entered with other helping souls such as the entities Joseph, Elizabeth, Zacharias, John the Baptist, and the Apostles. These entities demonstrated, through the panoramic play of their intertwined lives, the Love of Infinite, Intelligent, Creative Love. In this way they taught Creative Love with the hope that all restless and greedy souls who were reincarnated upon Earth-Eden at that time, and thereafter, would learn from their examples.

After great soul progression, entering Grace and being made perfect (as Infinite Intelligence) the Master became the "author of eternal salvation unto *all* who *obey* Him" (Infinite Intelligence) (Heb. 5:9). Salvation is gained not simply by saying the words "I believe in Christ," but by *obeying* the *teachings* of the Pathshower in daily thoughts, words and deeds. He did not want his followers to believe *in* him as something magical or mysterious. He wanted them to believe *with* him in Infinite, Intelligent, Creative Love. He wanted them to follow him in the example which he set of pure Trust in Infinite Intelligence to the degree of *knowing, understanding,* and *living* the way of Creative Love through the free will which is theirs.

The hope for your soul is as an anchor sure and steadfast both now and beyond the veil of needless tears. The Master reached perfection by constantly demonstrating Creative Consciousness to increasingly greater degrees. Then rising above the temporal, physical, bread and wine, to the splendid heights of a pure, constant thought-communion with Infinite, Intelligent, Creative Love through Creative Conscious thoughts. This progression results in Creative Conscious words and deeds, as the Pathshower demonstrated for you and all to follow.

The highest law of Grace is the reaching of the end of the reincarnative cycle; or in other words, the attaining of the state of Grace by having progressed sufficiently through purging oneself of selfishness. This is loving and learning without Karma (cause and effect), never having to go out again unless by choice to help guide or teach. *There are those among you!*, souls who have been *proven* pure, and are free of selfishness. Their presence will be explained in the next chapter of Soul Progression.

Individuals can gain progression through being born handicapped physically or mentally (although this need not be), but millions upon millions can gain a few or many steps up the staircase of progression toward Grace if they but smile at, talk to, visit with or care for such a soul. By your *deeds* you *shall* be known!!!

Reincarnation is the returning of a soul through rebirth into another human body upon Earth-Eden, thereby hopefully learning the lessons of soul progression by means of trial and error through cause and effect, or the constant meeting of "self." *This is not the best of ways in which to progress;* rather one should enter the highest law of Infinite Intelligence called Grace, in which one attains the nature of not being greedy, of not being materialistic, of not having the desire to reincarnate and re-enter the flesh again. This can be accomplished only when kindness, compassion, honesty, justice, respect, equality and concern for *all* others has become your primary way of life. This is living the Grace of Divine Love, being perfect as Infinite, Intelligent, Creative Love is perfect, wanting and needing to re-enter Earth-Eden no more. "Self meeting self" simply means recognizing all your regressions, misdeeds, shortcomings, and greed, accepting them as *wrong, wanting* to correct them, and then actually *living* a better life in Creative Consciousness.

Nevertheless, regardless of what your personal beliefs are concerning life after death, the important truth lies in what you do with this *life!* This life is very important! If you are a Christian or a Jew who believes that you live but one earthly life, and depending upon *how* you live it, that a judgment by God will decide whether you spend *all* eternity in either heavenly bliss or hell-fire torment—that belief makes this life *very* important!

If you are a Buddhist, or one who believes that you live many lives upon Earth-Eden, and depending upon how you lived the last one, a judgment by either Karma or yourself will determine in what situation you will find yourself in the future incarnation—that belief makes this life *very* important!

If you are an atheist who believes that this life is but a "one-shot-deal," with *no* hereafter—that belief makes this life *very* important!

This life *is* very important, *don't waste it, progress in soul!!!*

Chapter 6
Soul Progression

What *is* the soul? Is it that part of you which hopefully learns and progresses higher in each reincarnation? Is it composed of many lifetimes? Is it composed of many personalities? Is it that part of each of you which is also a part of Infinite Intelligence which has strayed, and is trying to return to Infinite Intelligence? *Yes*, it is all of these, and more! It is an idea-entity of Infinite, Intelligent, Creative Love. Hopefully, there will be progression beyond your present senses to help you become at-one with Infinite Intelligence. This, perhaps, may be as difficult to understand as it is to imagine an end to eternity or as difficult to understand as no end to enternity.

Taking stock of the spiritual growth in your life can help to elevate your soul. In daily meditation and reverie are found solutions of past and present problems; unfortunately, few meditate seriously, therefore wasting many years. *All* are standing on the threshold of spiritual growth, and from the bottom of despair can come some of your richest spiritual growth. It is spiritual growth that strengthens the soul which is to progress throughout eternity. "Let not your heart be troubled," (John 14:1) said the Galilean Teacher and Pathshower; therefore, believe in Him, in Infinite Intelligence and in yourself.

You are an individual, but you are also part of the whole of creation; this truth is exceedingly important. Infinite Intelligence knows not only the number of hairs on your head (Matt. 10:30), but your innermost thoughts; not as an eavesdropper, but as a concerned heavenly parent Who wishes Infinite Love for you and for every living creature. Love is the keynote and life eternal the harmonious chord. Open your heart to loving thoughts of kindness. Open your heart and let the sun shine in.

Diversity, simplicity and integrity are key factors in spiritual growth. It is all too easy to become stagnant with meditation, over-structured with religion and lazy with compassion and kindness. "Ponder not so much the material things, for neither do the lilies of the field" (Matt. 6:28), and are they not equally created by Love? Strive, however, toward the progression of your soul, for like the lily, Creative Love knows your needs before you ask, and with love shown equally to all, provides *all* that is necessary for the progression of your soul within a framework of loving laws structured for you as a guide to advancement within your abilities. Creative Love always keeps in mind your welfare and constantly gives you opportunities to open up your heart to giving and receiving help and love to and from others. This is the only purpose of life upon Earth-Eden: to progress enough to return to Creative Love, after having been "tried as gold in a furnace of love, having the dross of selfishness cast off, then standing pure in the highest of values, never having to go out again" (needing to reincarnate no more) (Wisdom 3:5-6).

Understanding the principles of the universal progression of life is an undertaking which presents itself in daily life through awareness; therefore, understanding one's own feelings and the feelings of one's neighbors is of utmost value. Your eternal world is not physical which shall pass away; rather, it is spiritual and eternal in existence because it has been created by, exists in, and continues to grow through concerned, non-tiring, Infinite Love. *This* is the essence of life! Those upon Earth-Eden who have not yet learned this, or who foolishly choose to reject it and continue to stumble along the path of life, will still have constant opportunities to learn. How fast one may progress depends upon the individual. Relatively few speed through this process simply because of the distractions of the physical world of materialism. Saints, prophets and wise-ones are few, but only a few are needed to teach *all* by *example*.

Neglect is one of the prime thieves in a family of thieves with lying and selfishness as its cousins. Although neglect is often unintentional, the results are nonetheless destructive. Neglect even exceeds its cousins in crime because it steals one of the most important things upon Earth-Eden...*time*! Give yourself an honest examination to see where neglect has caused you to fall short in your progression. Be it in your work, your studies, your marriage, or your relationships with others, realize that all are upon Earth-Eden for the progression of their souls and *nothing* else! Which path you choose to take on the physical map of life, with its endless roads of opportunity, is completely up to you. If the going gets a bit tough, remember that you are not alone. Ask for help from those souls upon Earth-Eden, those who have passed beyond the physical, or Creative Consciousness within you. You *shall* be helped because you were created for a special purpose which is to become perfect in soul even as Infinite Intelligence is perfect. This progression can only be achieved by demonstrating kindness, compassion, honesty, justice, respect and equality toward others and yourself, thus "reflecting the likeness in which you were created ages ago when the morning stars sang together" (Job 38:6-7).

"*Understanding*" is a key word in soul progression. An understanding of your soul in its *pure and free-from-self form* is gained as you daily, through thought, word and deed place yourself second, and those less fortunate first. Not a sparrow falls that Infinite Intelligence does not know. Not a soul in need who is helped by another, that Creative Love does not know. The radiance of that kindness reflects upon the good Samaritan.

You grow in understanding by doing; you grow faster by doing that which you may not care to do at that time. The negative feelings are soon overcome with that positive joy which good deeds always yield and radiate.

Your needs will be taken care of as you give more of yourself to others, with rewards both physical and spiritual. You may be helping an angel unaware, and you may someday be greatly surprised who that angel is. Follow your heart; it never lies to you, for that is where the Spirit of Holiness communes with you constantly, when you but open your heart and let the communication take place.

It is the meditations of the heart, the meditations of the mind and the meditations of the body which must be acceptable at all times. What are your meditations? Your desires are of little importance, but your goals are of great importance. Too often desires are mistaken for goals. When a person assumes the responsibility of another person who is less fortunate, to help that person grow in heart, mind and body, that is a goal of highest standards. Let not your heart be troubled, for your trust in Creative Love will heal all doubts and Infinite Intelligence will constantly supply spiritual and physical necessities to you and to those for whom you care.

"Seek and you will find, knock and the door will be opened for you" (Matt. 7:7). Give of yourself and you will receive much in return, for it is in giving that you receive, and it is in *trial* that you grow.

Kindness has no rival; therefore, who can be against you? Follow the compassion of your heart, for it leads upon the straight and narrow path which is ever upgrading, and though lonely at times, always rewarding. Creative Love makes possible the progression of your soul through works of kindness. All are called, but few have chosen to answer. You can make the few become many. It's up to you. What is your answer?

Realize that the entire universe strives to be in harmony with itself. Human greed is a major reason for discord. The harmony of Infinite Intelligent ideas can be yours. First you have the thought, then you speak the word and finally you begin to do the deed. If you do not mistake a desire for a goal, then all necessary elements for progression are yours as you take each step toward your goal. Although at times you may feel you are going through the valley of the shadow of doubt, you are not alone. You are being guided each step of the way. As great love is being shown on your part, greater Love is at your side. Relax, for it is by small yet constant steps that you ascend Jacob's ladder of Infinite Intelligence. All that you need will be supplied through Creative Love.

"Hiatus" means break, and that is what each of you often needs, a rest for the gathering of strength. If one is physically weak due to over-work, this can cause a deterioration of emotional strength resulting in doubt, anxiety or fear. If one is emotionally weak due to over-reacting to various situations which normally should bring progression to the soul, this can cause a deterioration of physical strength manifested in aches, pains, colds, or other dysfunctions. When these symptoms begin to show, it is best to take a mini-hiatus, be it for a few hours, days or weeks. If the situation is a major disorder, a longer hiatus is necessary. Often there is the need to physically relocate for a while, and to get away, be still, and quietly listen to that still small voice within, thus breaking the routine, getting out of a rut and meeting other refreshing souls in other refreshing places. But remember, *thought* is ever the builder; the result of what you are building depends upon what you are thinking. Thought can either make or break you, for you have been given freedom of thought. Use it progressively.

Do not linger too long in any place which you have outgrown, or you will become like a hermit crab who refuses to take on a new and larger shell, thus leaving itself without proper protection. Protect your body and your soul; for an unprotected or uncared-for house soon falls into disarray. Put your house in order! Give the same tender loving care to yourself and to others as you wish to receive, for such is the way to heaven.

When the heart smiles, its aches disappear. When its aches disappear, the body and soul can once again begin to progress with life. What causes the heart to smile is its own realization of its constant ability to overcome life's pains simply by knowing that Creative Love is omnipresent, *that* Truth shall make you free, if you but stop doubting. Rid yourself of blind faith and know that your cup of life is not only full with opportunity, but that it overflows. You cannot ask for more! Do not seek everything material with the false hope of simply enjoying this temporary, earthly life; rather, seek a spiritual life in order to eternally enjoy everything soulfully progressive.

"Eyes have not seen, ears have not heard, nor can you imagine what God (Creative Love) has prepared for *all*" (1 Cor. 2:9). Much can be brought forth and made manifest by those who demonstrate the reflection of Creative Love. This is progressing toward being perfect in soul as Infinite Intelligence is perfect! This is what some may refer to as the state of nirvana, paradise, heaven, Grace or the end of Karma and all reincarnations.

Where there is human love, there is Creative Love (reflection). Where there is no human love, there is no Creative Love (no reflection) but there is still Infinite Intelligence which is ever-present and constantly giving the opportunity for every living being to become a reflection of Creative Love for spiritual unfoldment of individual souls.

It is when one's eyes see a kind glance, when one's ears hear a harmonious chord, when one's thoughts ponder and realize, however momentarily, the things which Infinite Intelligence has prepared for all who love themselves, love their neighbors and that, in their daily deeds, they begin to demonstrate that at-one-ment (atonement) with Creative Love a bit more. This is religion, this is worship, this is returning from whence you come—going home!

Infinite Intelligence "neither slumbers nor sleeps" (Ps: 121:4). The force of Creative Love is never inactive. That Love, that Positiveness, that Forgiveness, that Concern, that Opportunity which is *the truth and the law, is always working properly* to endless capacity through Infinite Intelligence.

The minds of each of you are a reflection of Infinite Intelligence. Once you begin to think of yourself in that manner, you have reached a higher plateau of consciousness and understanding. You then begin to see yourself not only as a physical and mental creature, but as an enlightened being with unlimited possibilities. You begin to see the light at the end of the tunnel, however long it may seem to be. That light is the small spark, like that still small voice within, coming from the Light of Lights which enlightens you as you progress in mind toward ever-higher development. And what are higher thoughts? It would perhaps be easier to say what they are not! They are not anything which is not progressive, not loving, not positive, not forgiving, not concerned and not truthful.

As water quenches your thirst physically so can fulfilling Loving ways upon Earth-Eden quench your thirst for wrong, non-progressive deeds. Water is also for cleansing and needless to say, *all* can at times use a good mental scrubbing. Keeping your thoughts clean in turn will keep your words clean, which in turn will keep your deeds clean, thus you will have a progression and elevation of your entire being. You will be putting Creative Conscious ideas into operation. Treasure your soul; you have no greater priceless gem.

Chapter 7
Gem Progression

A gem collection of any size is a treasure. The larger the collection of gems, the greater is the value of the treasure. You have such a treasure. Count the gems you already have. Begin with the gem of your knowledge of Infinite, Intelligent, Creative Love, add to it your gem of faithful friendships, your gem of meditation, your gem of wanting progression for your soul, your gem of correcting past wrong, non-progressive acts and your gem of having the stains of false desires wiped clean. These are gems which you have gained through enlightenment.

Gem progression can be accomplished by disciplining yourself to the practice of silent prayer before a session of meditation. Meditate along a path which, in your mind's eye, leads you always higher, always toward more enlightenment and understanding. In meditation you will find an internal refuge which is the gem of inner peace that comes from the Infinite Source. You may then begin to realize the hardships which you may have caused others and feel as if you yourself have taken poison, for that is what wrongful deeds to others are. From this, learn restraint from any such deeds in the future.

There is also a fulfilling way to elevate your soul above past regression, by helping the needy, the poor, the ill, the imprisoned and by restoring the beauty of the scarred face of the planet Earth-Eden. Help to re-Eden-ize it. Earth-Eden is a gem of great value within the universe, although it may seem presently to some as Nazareth once seemed when the foolish asked, "What good could come out of Nazareth?"! (John 1:46)

Each living plant is a gem of Creative Love. Plant trees, flowers, bushes, orchards and vineyards for those who will come after you, since you did eat the fruit of orchards and did drink the wine of vineyards which were planted before your days. Then ask forgiveness for yourself, for the wrongs which you have committed against yourself, and grant it! Forget the deed, for you now have been elevated above it! Realize that forgiveness is also a gem in your now-growing collection of life progression. Understand these gems and learn to value them greatly, for here is found a storehouse of spiritual wealth for which no barns must be torn down in order for you to have more. If you truly learn the value of these gems, and live accordingly, you need not fear when your soul is called from this temporary earthly tent for self to meet self.

Look upon each species of creatures which fly in the air, swim in the waters, crawl beneath or walk upon Earth-Eden, as gems. Although they have not progressed to the enlightened stage of humans, they are gems of Creative Love which are progressing according to their own ways. Although they do not have souls of their own, they have what may best be termed "group souls" and, as they reincarnate, they will evolve soulfully into species of higher intelligence.

Many of you who are souls within human bodies today were the rebels who had gone astray because of self (selfishness). For *you* the Shepherd left the ninety and nine who had *not* rebelled and stayed faithful to God to bring you back into the fold. All of you constantly have the ability to progress to the pure and elevated state for which you were created eons ago when the morning stars sang together. Your souls are to progress higher and not be earth-bound rebels. The other creatures are in their proper place at this time, for Earth-Eden has a purpose in Infinite Intelligence. Unfortunately, some selfish souls became too materialistic and too flesh-conscious, forgetting their spiritual roots, and even forced their selfish influence upon the animals eons ago. Animals, according to their original purpose, were not meant to be fierce, rather the lamb was meant to lie down next to the lion.

A day in the courts of Infinite, Intelligent, Creative Love is as a billion eons, and a billion eons is as the twinkling of an eye in eternity. The lamb *will* lie down next to the lion as Isaiah foretold. Principal is firm! Principal is Infinite, Intelligent, Creative Love! Earth-Eden was not created to be defaced, littered and abused by humans. Birds were not created to be in cages, fish were not created to be placed in aquariums. Animals were not created to be in zoos or to be eaten by humans or each other. Vegetation was not created to be eaten by humans or animals. All of creation can be sustained by Creative Love alone. The present situation will not be changed overnight but shall come to pass. Human will is strong, but Creative Love is stronger. The fact is that Infinite Intelligence is perfect in understanding human weakness and compassionate toward that weakness.

The vicious beasts of the cave-man era were not created by Infinite Intelligence but by the wrong thoughts and greedy desires of free-willed souls. There were many other strange and un-needed creatures such as mixtures of the species, having grotesque results. Signs of these creatures such as the gargoyle and the sphinx can still be found in the ancient past. They did indeed exist along with other outrageous ideas (misuse of co-creation). These were results of desires rather than goals. It was purely lustful and selfish energy which had been misused. Unfortunately, greedy souls did enter into physical species eons ago because of their co-creative power. These weird and gruesome things were destroyed simply because they were not created properly and died by nature itself, for Earth-Eden was still in its early stages of formation. Remember, we are speaking in eons!

Living souls who entered the flesh were created by Infinite Intelligence with equal love, having their own valuable gems of purpose, which they had achieved through free will and co-creation. The other ninety-nine percent (countless trillions) have co-created properly according to Infinite Intelligence. Let us strongly remind you at this point that you were created in the likeness of Infinite Intelligence, and that is, in the *spirit* not in the physical; the physical is of your own doing!

The first story of the creation in the book of Genesis is nearer the truth than any other written account. Infinite Intelligence created you in spirit (a reflection of Infinite Intelligence), and it was in spirit in which souls were to dwell for a time upon Earth-Eden, but, because of self, greed, lust, power and ego, those co-creating souls entered into matter and disrupted the plan of Earth-Eden.

There is more knowledge available upon Earth-Eden today than in all the writings of the once great library of Alexandria. There also exists the (supposedly lost) Book of Jasher which is mentioned several times in the Old Testament, (nothing is lost in Infinite Intelligence), which tells of each soul being created in the eternity of Infinite Intelligence. "Jehovah (Infinite Intelligence) appeared in Eden (Earth-Eden), and created man (souls), and made him (them) to be an image (likeness) of his (Creative Love's) own *eternity*" (Jasher 1:11). The likeness of Creative Love's own eternity! This was spiritual creation of eternal souls. Let us remind you at this point that Earth-Eden has an entirely different purpose than supporting physical human life, which *will* be fulfilled! We will explain this with greater detail in the chapter on Creative Progression.

In the Book of Revelation, which is the last book of the New Testament, are mentioned one hundred forty-four thousand souls who will live upon Earth-Eden after much is said and done! It is a parable of truth. For although the number is a general number which can vary one way or the other, it speaks the truth regarding what Earth-Eden will eventually become when *all* humans have progressed soulfully to the perfection of their original purpose which is to leave the physical and be purely spiritual again; Heaven. Then Earth-Eden will be properly cared for by a certain number of these souls of purely spiritual form of highest progression. Blessed are the meek and pure in heart for they shall see Creative Love and inherit Earth-Eden. You see, dear stray sheep, Earth-Eden will be a place for the highest of souls to progress even higher in Infinite Intelligence! A retreat for those souls of all spiritual species which have progressed to the point of, "having been tried as gold in a furnace of Creative Love with the dross of self-greed burned off to the perfection of standing in golden atonement, becoming at-one with Infinite Intelligence" (Wisdom 3:5-6)!

This is the heavenly goal for each of you. This is where sisters, brothers, mothers, fathers, sons, daughters are to dwell in harmony. Perfect harmony. Not as physical individuals of the family relationship of your last incarnation, but as spiritual souls of advancement, where no one is given or taken in marriage (although various forms of sex, partnerships, soul-mergers or other relationships do exist in the Second Realm). No sin, no sickness, no aging, no death, *no human greed*!

Know that Infinite, Intelligent, Creative Love gives you free will, and *constantly, patiently* guides you toward perfection. "*Today* is your day to begin your salvation" (2 Cor. 6:2)! *Today* is great with love! *Today, begin to meet self*, for in the future your soul can progress beyond your present comprehension! "Today you see as in a clouded mirror; eventually you will see clearly (through enlightenment), face to face" (1 Cor. 13:12)! There shall be a new heaven, and a new Earth-Eden, which shall never pass away, but rather will be filled with kindness and justice!

Chapter 8
Justice Progression

What is God? God is complete justice, *all* in all, the great I Am of which you are a part, from whence you came, where to you should be trying to return. God is We, Us, All. God is idea, God is love, God is powerful, God is spirit, God is omnipresent, God is omnipotent, God is most of the titles given to God in the scriptures of many religions. God is father, God is mother, God is soul, God is perfect in all God's actions, God is thought, God is first, God is the ultimate rule of action, God is tears, God is smiles, God is compassion, God is kindness, God is perfect, God is good. We could go on endlessly giving you titles for God, trying in the limited usage of words to define God but, basically, God is Infinite, Intelligent, Creative Love.

When you humans think of God, to many of you, one god comes to mind. For some, many gods come to mind; for others, the idea of a trinity or triune god comes to mind. All these concepts can allow for individual soul progression.

To think of God as many gods is understandable in that there are many souls who have given up self to such a degree as to have risen high above the materialistic human concept as have those who have led saintly lives, thereby demonstrating their loving desire to become perfect after the change called death to the point of at-one-ment with Infinite Intelligence and thus becoming more aware of Creative Love.

To think of God as triune, in being the Father, the Son and the Holy Spirit, is understandable in that God is the *spirit of holiness* (which is the best terminology for God besides Infinite, Intelligent, Creative Love). God in the father is the true mother, the true parent of concern. God in the son is the true daughter, the true offspring as each of you are God's creation and hopefully progressing higher in soul.

It is understandable to think of God as one god in that Infinite

Intelligence is diversified in unity, plus this knowledge also offers each individual soul opportunity for higher progression.

Think of Creative Love as the source of *all* life, as a spring-fed lake which brings forth pure, cool, refreshing water, without which you human beings could not have the temporary physical life which you do presently experience. This lake endlessly meets *all* your needs! It is uniquely shaped with its varied, patterned circumference, and its shore seems to some as many shores (many gods), to some as three sided (triune god) and yet to others as one (one god). All three concepts are understandable because of the diversity of the lake which flows over in many places, thus creating brooks, creeks and rivers, which may be seen as the various religions of the world. It is the lowly soul who sees only the differences of the religions, thinking that one is superior to all others; but it is the progressed soul who sees the source of Infinite Intelligence in all these tributaries.

As a pebble when thrown into a pond causes ripples to flow from the center and gradually to become larger and larger until they reach every inch of the pond's diversified shore, so is everyone's need for soul progression constantly being met by Infinite Intelligent, Creative Love. God is Creative Love and Infinite Intelligence which is *equally just* to *all.*

How does this justice work for you? Lo, we shall reveal unto you a mystery; there are no accidents! How can there be if Perfection created *all*? Perfection's creations could not for even one slight second be accidental! Even in the material existence upon Earth-Eden, this is fact. First, take a long meditative look at the word "Creative" and then a long meditative look at the word "Consciousness." Place them together as "Creative Consciousness" and you will begin to understand.

The entity known as the Master Teacher Jesus did truly walk your planet and demonstrated Creative Consciousness more than any other human. The Master was, is, and will be for ages to come, the Pathshower and the Example for all. That Galilean had progressed to such a degree as to be called God by some, but he himself said "Greater things than I, you can do" (John 14:12). A puzzle? No. The Pathshower was simply trying to explain that you are all a part of Infinite

Intelligence and should be striving to progress constantly. The only way to do this is through the good virtues which you know in your heart; kindness, compassion, honesty, justice, respect and equality; for this is the *only* way Infinite Justice deals with you.

Think of the Master as being truly a person of love and peace and *not* the person who is often depicted in the Gospels as threatening people with hellfire, "coming as a double-edged sword to divide families, not to bring peace" (Matt. 10:34,35). The Loving Pathshower was a much kinder individual than some of the writers of the scriptures imply; of most importance was his exemplary life and his compassionate teachings.

Not all religious books of the various overstructured religions are totally the word of Infinite Intelligence, but like many books through the ages (as this one), are a mingling of the thoughts of Infinite Intelligence with those of souls (of various levels of progression) made manifest in words. They can be holy writ only when they create a holy situation or result in kindness, compassion, honesty, justice, respect and equality thus creating progression between humans and Infinite Intelligence, between humans and each other, between humans and all other creatures, plants and nature.

Others besides the Master had demonstrated Creative Consciousness but never to such a high degree. Elijah in the Old Testament demonstrated Creative Consciousness when he resurrected a little boy (1 Kings 17:17-24), as did a widow in the New Testament when she gave her last two coins to the poor; thus she gave her *all* (Mark 12:42-44). You all must strive to become Lovingly Creative. When you falter, this is where justice comes in. Remember Creative Love paves the way so that not one soul should perish. We can easily add that Infinite Justice paves the way for every soul's progression. Therefore Infinite Love, in Its Infinite Wisdom, allows you to have free will; thus, the law of justice has been set in motion and *you* shall reap what *you* have sown. "Not one whit nor tittle" (Matt. 5:18) shall in any way pass without being recorded in the Third and higher Realms in what is best known as the Akashic Records.

Your individual record for this incarnation is recorded to the smallest jot, not out of vengeance, but out of loving, kind, concerned, caring justice. Remember, Infinite Love knows your needs (and thoughts, be they good or not) before you ask, and with equal Love provides *all* that which is necessary for the progression of your soul within a framework of Loving Laws structured for you as a guide to advancement within your abilities. Infinite Intelligence always keeps in mind your welfare and constantly gives you opportunities to open your heart to giving and receiving help and love to and from others.

You have read this before in the chapter on Soul Progression, but now you *must* begin to do something about it. *Learn it! Live it!* For you shall truly keep returning upon Earth-Eden to work out your deeds until you have been "tried as gold in a furnace of love, after having the dross of selfishness cast off, then standing pure in the highest of values, never having to go out again!" (Wisdom 3:5-6). Sound familiar? Wonder where you heard that before? *Learn it! Live it!* The only way peace upon Earth-Eden can be achieved is through *you*! It must begin by small yet constant steps for each entity to realize that Jesus saves you not simply by your vocally professing him to be the savior; rather, you are saved through your living by his *example*!

For God's sake, *wake up*! Be like Infinite Justice, never slumbering, sleeping, (Ps. 121:4), nor kidding yourself concerning your deeds. Grow up! You must lead a better life! That's how you are saved! There is *no proxy*! Remember it was Jesus who said not everyone who calls him "Lord, Lord" will mean too much to him; rather, it would be asked, "Who are you? I know you not, for you did not do good works (of Creative Love). When did you visit those in jail, the sick and the oppressed? Whatsoever you did to the least of these your brothers and sisters, you did unto me" (Matt. 25:44-45) (You did unto yourself). The whole idea of the Master Pathshower's life was to help the souls upon Earth-Eden to stop reincarnating and enter Grace through their deeds as did he. No one can progress for you. No one can return to Infinite Justice for you. No one can change your heart but you. Creative Love is one hundred percent behind you, and the Pathshower is an ever guiding example; follow it! What upon Earth-Eden are you waiting for? Be guided by just principles and just actions, for is not Infinite

Intelligence Just Principle, Just Action?

Take a good long look at Love's creations. The heavens, the seas, the mountains, the valleys, the deserts, the lakes, the fields, the rivers, the trees, the planets, the animals, the fish, the heat, the cold, the breezes, the clouds, the moon, the sun, the countless stars, the rainbow, and *you*! Read that through again—and *you*! Can you begin to imagine the immensity of creation? Take time to do so. (You take time to go to the bathroom every day!!) *Take time to think about your place in creation!!* We are not giving you any riddles like those of Nostradamus! Creative Love is Loving-Justice, Caring-Justice! So loving, so caring as to have given you free will with guidelines. Should you steal, you must learn not to. Should you kill, you must learn not to. Should you lie, you must learn not to. Should you covet, you must learn not to! *How* depends entirely on you! It is easier for a rope to go through the eye of a needle than it is for a greedy person to progress (Mark 10:25), and this is where reincarnation comes in, this is where justice comes in! You will reincarnate time after time in various situations until you have learned your lessons, until you have met self. If you reject Grace, the highest Law of Infinite Intelligence, you will answer to Karma, the second highest Law of Infinite Intelligence! No use blaming the devil, because Infinite Intelligence has no competition. The only difference between devil and evil is the letter "d"!

In Chapter 5, Reincarnative Progression, you read that the highest Law, Grace, is the reaching of the end of the reincarnative cycle—in other words—having attained the state of Grace, thus having progressed enough by purging oneself of selfishness to continue to love and learn without cause and effect (Karma), and never having to go out again (reincarnate upon Earth-Eden,) (Rev. 3:12) unless, by choice, to help, guide, or teach others. There *are* "those among you," those souls who have been proven pure in freedom from selfishness! You also have read in that chapter that the second highest Law of Karma automatically goes into action when the first and preferred Law of Grace is rejected or neglected. Remember, the Master said that greater things than he has done can be done by others (John 14:12). There is *no* Law which says anyone *must* reincarnate. It is by one's own actions that the reincarnation occurs. It *is* possible *not* to reincarnate. All things are possible in Creative Love. It's up to each individual soul as to how it plans to live upon Earth-Eden. Remember, Earth-Eden should not be your goal; it is not your home.

(The old) "heaven and (the old) Earth-(Eden) shall pass away" (Matt. 24:35), and where will *you* be? There shall come a time when there no longer will be a need for this school upon Earth-Eden. Creative Love will be pure in *all* without the need of matter, only pure spirit, the demonstration of the Highest Principle for *all*! When will this be? The peace upon Earth-Eden, the goodwill to all will be the beginning of the eternal millennium of love. How close is it? How much have you given of your *abundance* to those in need, physically and spiritually? How much have you given of your *need*? When will you begin to give your *all*?? *That* is when it will happen! You really own nothing; don't fool yourself, don't tear down your barns to build larger barns, for tomorrow your soul may be called in for inspection (Luke 12:18,20). Rather meditate upon the following: "I give to Creative Love but its own, and *all* I have is from Creative Love." Don't try to store, bank, hide, or bury your talents, your treasures, your gifts, for there your heart is also!! It is only by kindness, compassion, honesty, justice, respect, and equality that your soul can progress to its fullest extent. To hell as to heaven with Karma, to heaven only with Grace. The path to Grace becomes more straight, more narrow and more rewarding as you travel along.

It is not necessary for us to cite various evidences of reincarnation. This book is not to be one of recorded case histories for there are enough of those already; rather, this is to be a book which will set the record straight, and help your soul to progress. Reincarnation, as gravity, does exist even if you do not believe in either; however, acceptance of this truth is certainly an aid.

How can you stop Karma and enter Grace? "Judge not unrighteously, so that you will not be judged unrighteously "(Matt. 7:1). Do unto others as you wish them to do unto you. All are your brothers and sisters; all colors, races, religions, nations, political systems, ages and all of the various sexual orientations; all the beautiful, ugly, rich, poor, wise, stupid, kind, cruel, honest, dishonest; all are your brothers and sisters. How many times must this message be preached? You *are* your neighbor's keeper (Gen. 4:9)! Perhaps you were once a queen and next will be a doctor. Perhaps you were once a thief and next will be born minus what you have stolen. Perhaps you were once unjust and next will suffer injustice, or are suffering it now! This is Karma.

This does not say that all unfortunates are being punished; remember the example from Chapter 5, Reincarnative Progression, where the man born blind could have *chosen* to have been born blind so that Creative Love could have been made manifest in him through the Pathshower's demonstration of Creative Consciousness, thus gaining soul progression from his loss of sight and ending his time under Karma, entering Grace, therefore needing to reincarnate no more.

Let us remind you of those who care for handicapped souls. If they labor merely for the pay, they neither lose nor gain. If they treat these souls poorly and perform their tasks without heart, *beware*! This surely is the road downhill to a *severe* Karma. Those who, in their hearts, with their words and deeds, do truly *help* these needy souls will indeed become more perfect in soul as Creative Love is perfect.

The line in the Old Testament which reads, "Vengeance is mine saith the Lord" (Heb. 10:30) has been revised to "Justice is mine saith the Lord." It should be revised to "Vengeance belongs to no one, and justice to everyone." As we have said before, words often seem inadequate and lose or change their meanings as time passes; therefore, books such as this are written with the wisdom of the ancients rephrased into the idioms of the present. When you are reading the scriptures (you do at times, don't you?) and do not fully understand them, look for one or two sentences that may be close to your needs, and change a word or two to help you judge your own actions better.

When you judge yourself and others, or judge situations, always keep in the back of your mind one question: "What would Creative Love have me do?" With that sort of intelligent guidance, you most certainly cannot stray knowing that this kind of judgment comes from justice, that is, if you *obey* that still small voice within you which never lies to you (1 Kings 19:12). Even though you may not always care for the answer when you realize that it will inconvenience you, listen to it, follow it! You can always have communion with that still small voice which comes from the only *source* and *always* has the correct answer. Simply take time out to pay attention to Love's creation around you. Recall from earlier in this chapter, "All the beauty—the rainbow, and you." Remember, Creative Love paves the way so that no soul should perish. Your neighbors are your brothers and sisters. Earthly life is often just a few short eighty summers, then what will happen to you?

Privileges in trust, privileges in friendships, privileges in judgments are *not* to be taken except in extreme situations and under guarded thought. Take not lightly any bond between yourself and another person or between yourself and Infinite Intelligence. Be that other person a friend who trusts you or a defendant who awaits the decision of a jury of which you are a member, the result must be an honest one, for if it is not, you *will* reap the harvest of the bitter deeds which you have sown. Some mistakes, simply because of their nature, are almost impossible to erase, such as sentencing an innocent person to prison for many years. Such cases fall under *severe* Karma. Poor, bad and even completely false judgments given out by juries create a collective guilt. *Much* Karma is still being worked out even today by those who were on councils, or in power as far back as the time of the Galilean Master, and even centuries before. Justice is Law; it is Infinite Principle's Law even unto the last comma or period. Learn from these teachings and follow the Galilean fisher of souls, your brother, who did not die in vain.

That Galilean fisher of souls had reached Creative Consciousness to a higher degree than any human ever achieved! In this, his last incarnation, he accepted Infinite Justice's offer to demonstrate the overcoming of the flesh through example to a troubled world. He was "tried as gold in a furnace of Love after having the dross of selfishness cast off, then stood pure in the highest of values, never having to go out" upon Earth-Eden again except by choice (Wisdom 3:5-6). He proved the spiritual to be superior to the physical. He conquered the corruptible body through his Creative Conscious ways of following Infinite Intelligence, thus transformed by himself into the incorruptible body. By his own words, he *will* return again, "I shall come again and call mine unto me" (John 14:3). He most certainly *will* return. The time no one but Infinite Intelligence knows, the reason is known to all—to usher in the era which the Pathshower demonstrated while upon Earth-Eden—*peace*. Not necessarily the era mentioned in the book of Revelations, for there need *not* be that doom if people but elevate their ways above greed and material possessions, to kindness, compassion, honesty, justice, respect, equality and forgiveness.

Chapter 9
Forgiveness Progression

"Those sins which you forgive are forgiven, but those sins which you do not forgive are held" (Matt. 16:19 & 18:18) taught the Master in Creative Consciousness. And they are surely held, and held firm not only for the one who sinned, but also for the one sinned against. This is an often misunderstood statement of the Galilean Teacher. Let go; it does no one any good to hang on. The Master was not speaking about any special religious system or any titled person. No third party can really forgive you your sins, only the person whom you sinned against can. If the person whom you have sinned against has passed from Earth-Eden, a third party can only help you to speak meditatively to them to ask for forgiveness. Stop fooling yourself! Once you have been forgiven, that's not the end of it either; you *must* repent from doing it again, and you *must* make up the wrong which you have committed, if possible. Contrition and rectification are a *must.*

"Forgive us our trespasses as we forgive those who trespass against us" (Matt. 6:12) *"As we forgive"*—you cannot be forgiven if you do not *also* forgive. Forgiveness and contrition go hand in hand. Show kindness to that handicapped person whom you know, for you may be surprised as to what Karma *you* may be working off from a past incarnation; you may be surprised as to what a wonderful opportunity lies before you, and you may be surprised as to what Karma you may be helping the *handicapped* person to overcome from past incarnations.

Forgiveness *must* go into action as soon as possible when kindness has been neglected or rejected by the other person or persons. The Creative Example was demonstrated by the Pathshower in a most heart-rending way at the end of his last reincarnation upon Earth-Eden when those of low soul progression wrongfully tortured and slaughtered this Teacher of teachers. Through their greed and ignorance, they thought that they could have their will done rather than that of Creative Love. He cried for their forgiveness saying that they knew not what they were doing. (Lk. 23:34) He forgave them immediately, for he knew that it was their ignorance of Loving Intelligence through which they executed their heinous act!

It is important that each one of you tries to follow the example of the Nazarene who showed and taught the way by word and example. His teachings of turning the other cheek, of giving even your coat when only being asked for your shirt, of going the extra mile are all forms of forgiveness.

How do you forgive a person who has taken from you a position which you cherished, loved and helped to create? How do you forgive a person who has released you from your employment after a generation of faithful service, leaving you in need of funds? The answer is easy, the consummation often very difficult and painful. You forgive as soon as possible, as soon as your heart begins to heal. How is this done? It is done with the healing-balm of love within that broken heart which is still there, ever mending, ever reflecting the greater Creative Love of Infinite Intelligence. It is done slowly by replacing the hurt with sincere hope of spiritual growth for your offender, to keep the grapes of wrath out of your own vineyard of life. For such grapes provide no wisdom-wine, rather sour grapes provide only vinegar, which when mixed with gall makes no communion cup. Therefore, with the wisdom of the past and the hope for the future for both yourself and your offender, you place your trust in Creative Love and begin to forgive.

The scriptures quote the Son of Bethlehem to have said: "Love your enemies, forgive those who falsely persecute you," (Matt. 5:44), but the scriptures do not finish that story or tell how it is to be done. One way is to ignore the differences between you and your enemy; rather, see all that which you have in common. Your enemy does not like to freeze, neither do you. Your enemy does not like to starve, neither do you. Your enemy does not like to be ill, neither do you. Your enemy hopefully has some love within, hopefully so do you. And upon that love for mother, father, sister, brother, friend or mate, you can begin to build a common bond, begin to forgive, begin to break down your differences and begin to progress.

When there is no forgiveness, the body suffers anything from tenseness and headaches to major disorders and in extreme cases, even the passing of the soul out of the body resulting in the change called death. The positive reaction upon the body after forgiveness takes place is the opposite; it may take time for adjustment but it most certainly will come. The physical and emotional results affect both the offender and the offended. Remember, body and soul work intertwined, but whereas the body will last for only a few short decades, the soul will continue throughout eternity.

When the Master Teacher was asked by those who heard him teach how many times one is to forgive, they wondered if it should be seven or seventy times. As people who were greatly attracted to endless rules and regulations which they mistakenly called religious laws, they had hopes of adding one more to the list. However, to their disappointment, his answer was not what they had expected. "Seventy times seven" (Matt. 18:22), or endlessly was his answer. Without their realizing it, he had truly given them a rule of Infinite Principle. You *must* forgive, lest that which you feared most or forgave least will come upon you. Just for one dire moment, suppose that Creative Love would not forgive!! Where would your future hang?

Take time *now*. Write that letter, make that visit and forgive those whom you have not yet forgiven. If they have passed on, speak to them and ask for forgiveness, lest the day shall come when it may seem to become impossible to do so. You are a reflection of Forgiving Love. Reflect, forgive, then take a deep breath, feel better, feel loved, feel at-one-ment with your fellow human beings and with Infinite Love; for in these actions you truly take many steps homeward.

Each soul upon Earth-Eden must admit and face their wrongs in order to advance higher. They must "meet themselves" (self) at one point or another. When will it be for you? Will it be now or will you postpone it until later, taking the chance of building up more wrong Karma rather than entering Grace? "*Today* is the day of salvation"

(2 Cor. 6:2). Placed before you is good and evil, which will you choose, the real truth, or the nothingness of the lie? You come under your own rod of chastisement, no one else's. Choose wisely by following the Master along the path to Grace *now*! May forgiveness progression become your idea.

Chapter 10
Idea Progression

As a person thinks, so the person is! Thought is ever the builder. Penetrate the eggs of any species and there is a disturbance or destruction of those eggs; so it is with pure meditative ideas. To keep a thought pure, there must be no penetration of the embryonic idea or it will be disturbed or destroyed.

Meditate, breathe properly, relax, then weed out the wrong thoughts from the garden of your mind so that they do not become dried and needlessly stored, taking up valuable space which could be allotted for soul progression rather than regression. Often your mental-garden needs attentive weeding.

Each human has the ability to think millions upon millions of ideas and every single one of those ideas can be a progressive one. Infinite Intelligence has an endless number of ideas, each one of which is completely filled with loving opportunities, and every soul is one of those ideas!

"Seek and you *shall* find, knock and doors *shall* be opened" (Matt. 7:7). These eternal words of wisdom have rung out through the ages from civilization to civilization. They form the key which unlocks all doors to personal and collective progression. "Seeking" and "knocking" means "*motivation*." Even a mustard seed has motivation and uses it!! Motivation does not simply come by asking! Infinite Intelligence knows your thoughts and needs even before you do with the opportunities already there. Seek! Follow-up! Knock! Open the countless doors of idea-progression.

Like the birds of the air who seek their seeds of life, so you must seek your idea-seeds of life. As each seed which is planted and nurtured correctly can grow into any one of millions of types of plants, so can ideas if planted and nurtured correctly grow into realities. However, you must begin weeding in your mental garden at the very beginning of a new adventure, so as to keep a firm root, a steady vine, pruning non-productive idea-shoots, and eventually reaping the harvest of fine wine on the vine of motivation. Wisdom-wine! "For wine maketh glad the heart of man (humans)" (Ps. 104:15), states the Old Testament, and wisdom maketh glad the hearts of many.

Make your mind a garden of paradise, of reflection, of meditation, of relaxation, of beauty, of love, of forgiveness, of growth, of peace. In such a garden where you would walk like that of Eden, and would gladly enter in to meet with Creative Love, a garden wherein the lamb of kind ideas will lie down next to the lion of strength in peace without the mental conflict of selfishness. And in that garden have a temple of learning for yourself wherein you can often enter joyously to learn more of the ways of Infinite, Intelligent, Creative Love, which the Master himself taught while he trod upon Earth-Eden. For he kept his word when he said, "I will not leave you alone as orphans, but will send you another comforter in that of the Spirit of Truth" (John 14:16-18), which indeed will *always* meet with you in the temple of the garden of your heart, if you will but be aware of *that* Presence.

Nurture each infant idea as a bud and each flower as the blossoming fulfillment of that idea, as they orderly grow along the well-maintained, sure, foundational paths of Truth. Constantly uproot the weeds of greed and selfishness, thus maintaining the mental garden of your heart. The gate to your garden is not missing a handle on the outside as some artists portray it to be, with the Master knocking and waiting for you to open from the inside; rather, it is a gate with no lock at all. It swings open quite freely and permits constant and easy access for *you* to enter therein, to meet with Creative Love which is constantly present in that tabernacle. For there, in the tabernacle of your temple-heart, you will learn that Creative Love alone is your bread of life-growth and the wine of wisdom-forgiveness which you can receive daily. Listen to the guidance in the silent meditation of your heart. For this is what communion really is.

Before you eat any meal, do as the Master asked; remember him and his teachings. Let your thrice daily breaking of bread and wine (your breakfast, lunch and supper) be reminders to follow the Pathshower's example. Before each meal commune with the Infinite Supplier in giving silent thanks for the food before you, and for the animals and vegetation which gave up their physical lives so that you might for a time have physical life. Commune with thanks and gratitude to the Infinite Supplier, from where *all* things come. In that garden you can weed out the false weed-idea of fear. Fear is nothing more or less than lack of trust in Infinite Intelligence. If you do not trust Infinite Intelligence, where would you foolishly place trust? In mammon? "No one can serve two masters; for either they will hate the one and love the other, or they will stand by and be devoted to the one and despise the other. You cannot serve God (Infinite, Intelligent, Creative Love) and mammon (materialism)" (Matt. 6:24). Rather plant the grass of seed-ideas all around your garden, since "If Creative Love is for us, what can be against us?" (Rom. 8:31). Upon that sod of pleasantness, make your needed occasional retreat.

Let the pillars of your mental temple be as the tall cedars of Lebanon, firm with progressive ideas, supporting the ever heavenward, ever celestial, ever soaring ideas of Creative Love. Keep the aisles of your mental temple clean from the aging dust of malice, for it is your very own personal Holy of Holies which can be reached only through your silent meditation. Let the music of your Holy of Holies be reverent, joyful and above all harmonious as that of the music of the spheres of the universe themselves. Heaven is harmonious! Think about that for a moment; could you ever imagine heaven to not be harmonious? And heaven as harmony is yours for the taking if you but turn from the disharmony, the discord of your daily experiences. If this seems difficult, then this is where your meditation becomes essential.

It is a *must* for each and every soul to enter the temple-heart. It is there where you have the opportunity of "meet thine own self;" it is there where you can honestly make an evaluation of yourself. Remember, "Where your treasure is, there your heart is also" (Matt. 6:21). "*All* shall pass away" (Matt. 24:35) (including your earthly clay-vessel) except the "Word" which is Creative Love, which is Infinite Intelligence. You are a part of the Word and need only to try a bit more each day to progress and let the "Light of the World" reflect and become the light in your temple-heart that Love, that Creative Consciousness which the Pathshower taught and lived. Let it shine before you in deeds of kindness, compassion, honesty, justice and equity as a guide for you and others to follow.

Remember that your thoughts and desires are all known to Infinite Intelligence. Be careful what you crave lest it should come upon you; rather, let your thoughts, your desires, your cravings, your constant meditation be thus: "Infinite, Intelligent, Creative Love, thank You for being and thank You for letting me be. Thank You for the constant opportunity of oneness with You, with all my fellow humans, with all that lives, with all which You in Your Infinite Wisdom have created. Thank You for keeping me in mind, for helping me overcome my failings, and thank You for keeping the door of reformation constantly open, now and even after the change called death. I shall try through the example of the Galilean Pathshower to lose 'self' unto Your ways. Amen."

Let your benediction be a constant reminder that you are your "brother's, (your sister's, your mother's, your father's and your neighbor's) keeper" (Gen. 4:9). You are keeper of the Truth, that which Infinite, Intelligent, Creative Love blesses *you* with. "Do unto others" (Matt. 7:12) as Creative Love does unto you. The garden of your heart can be as the scripture verse says, "Eye has not seen, ear has not heard" (1 Cor. 2:9), nor can one imagine what the Infinite Supplier alone has prepared for you to use properly. Forget not, that in past lives, in the present life or in lives to come you may have met or may yet meet in opposite situations of Karma.

For the refreshment of soul then, walk through your mental garden alone, while the dew of spiritual refreshment is still on the roses of constant love, and there meet yourself in Creative Love and dispose of your thorns of pride. Roses of beauty surround you, if you but take the time to notice them in the mental garden of your temple-heart; you can do this while being meditatively cognitive.

Chapter 11
Cognitive Progression

I, Curt, wish to insert a personal note, for it was at this point that I began to increase the ability to speak in an enlightened state of consciousness while lying down. I never personally cared for mediumship for myself. As a youngster at the age of fourteen, I was encouraged to experiment with "cabinet work," or, in other words, seance mediumship. Various mediums told me that I had the ability; therefore, it was tried. I was successful but did not care for working in the dark, and would often have severe headaches afterwards; the result was that I refused to continue.

As much as I admired the work of known psychics, I disliked the idea of being totally unconscious. Although many psychics encouraged me through the years to make use of my psychic abilities, I felt that if I were to do any special work, the manner in which it should to be done should reflect light and consciousness.

As I finished writing the chapter of Idea Progression, the writing continued with a personal note to me, instructing me to attempt to receive information through inspirational speaking as well as through inspirational writing while in an enlightened state of consciousness (in which I would not be unconscious).

Then in a lighted room I lay down, prayed, meditated and, after breathing deeply several times, cleared my mind and experienced the familiar trance-like feeling as in an inspirational writing session. Without another person present as a conductor, I gave myself the instructions, I asked myself questions. It sounded very strange to distantly hear my own voice steadily answer in a positive, authoritative, yet kind manner. In a way it seemed similar to inspirational writing in that I heard the word a split second before I spoke it, often wondering where it was going in thought and what would follow.

I now am able to easily receive information not only by writing but also by speaking without being unconscious and not in darkness! The following is a tape-recorded transcript of my first inspiration speaking session while in an enlightened state of consciousness without the aid of a conductor. Realize that the information comes from the same source as the inspirational writing.

"Everlasting, Creative Love, I come to You bidding to do Your Will and Your Work. Guide me as I attempt for the first time to make communication alone with the same source in inspirational speaking as I have through inspirational writing. Please keep my body and soul free from any danger and let me awaken refreshed and protected. In the name of Creative Consciousness. Amen.

"Clear the mind."

The mind is clear.

"Please go to where, to whom, to what in order to obtain the following information and tell me when you are ready."

We are ready!

"Please give me whatever information you feel is necessary for the next chapter of this book."

Perhaps the first topic of interest at this point should be an understanding of that which has happened to all of you in the physical. Regardless whether you accept it or not, the body is but a clay vessel and the entity, the personality, is but a day in the life of the soul. The soul has many personalities, known as many birth experiences, or what you refer to as reincarnations. This may seem difficult for some to grasp because you are still thinking on a three dimensional level, in a materialistic idea-structure, upon Earth-Eden as you know it.

The soul of our channeling instrument Curt, who is presently speaking, is as old as time, as are the souls of many others who have so chosen at one time to leave, to go out and search into matter, to understand and experience the varied limited feelings and sensations of matter. Through years of travel, many have learned and have progressed, but that manner is a limited way. For where is the best place of learning? In the spiritual courts of Infinite Intelligence (Ps. 65:4)! Keep in mind that you all must return if you are in any way to become part of the whole in a serious manner again. This entity, our channeling instrument, who is speaking at this time, has reached very high extents, but unfortunately, at times has simply forgotten the power which is within. Be not afraid; ask, it shall be given you, but also be prepared to receive it. Therefore, be careful as to what you ask.

We also say to our channeling instrument, Curt, that as for your friends, who were in the various different fields of the clergy, they were not necessarily examples, they were not necessarily wrong. Many of them were clergy simply because in past lives they could not understand Infinite Intelligence themselves, and only by coming back as leaders of overstructured religions, by telling others how to live, could they themselves gain the strength to believe what they were saying. This is not the case here. You are love, you are kindness. You shall go from love to Love, from kindness to Kindness.

This is the first of this type of session wherein you speak while in an enlightened state of consciousness with no conductor needed. Is this not an answer to what you have been asking for since you were young and doubted the psychics at the Spiritualist camps? And though they were spattered with charlatans, there was that certain percentage who were grand sensitives. Remember that as you are sensitive, you are also capable of stumbling and falling. Ever keep in mind from whence your guidance comes. Ever keep in mind that it is the sincere desire of Creative Love for you to return home, and if you have chosen to guide others along the way, so be it. The false notion you have had, that one must begin no later than the age of thirty or forty is wrong, for there is no time limit. Your psyche, your understanding, the opening up of the lotus-of-love within your solar-plexus, is beyond, as Tennyson said, "your wildest dreams."

We would at this time suggest that you do much more meditation. Practice in this manner, preferably upon an empty stomach, but reverse your position. Be it with your head toward the north and your feet toward the south, rather than the position which you are in now. When you go into an enlightened state of consciousness, you can go into higher realms than this, the Third Realm which you are reaching at this time.

We know that you have questions as to who We are and why the plural. That shall all be answered in due time. Let us keep you with this one thought in mind. *Me* is *I. I* is *I Am. I Am* is *Us* and *Us* is *We*.

We are finished. Return refreshed and rested to normal consciousness with the blessings of Love. Awaken, this is not a dream.

I can't begin to find the words with which to express my feelings about this inspirational speaking session. I listened to the tape many times. I was in wonderment; for although it was my voice, it was not really me speaking. I truly trust my Angelic Guides and thank them for their love and patience and will attempt another session at a later date.

Chapter 12
Dream Progression

"Your sons and your daughters shall prophesy, your old men shall dream dreams, your young men shall see visions" (Joel 2:28). These are the rewards spoken of by Joel in the Old Testament which shall be outpoured upon those souls who fill their lives with the Spirit of Holiness. Prophecies, visions and dreams are closely related in that they are signs given unto you entities upon Earth-Eden from souls in higher realms to help guide you back to God. Dreams are spoken of many times in both the Old and the New Testaments. Joseph, the husband of Mary, obeyed his dreams. Joseph of the Old Testament interpreted the dreams of Pharaoh. Jacob dreamed that he saw a ladder with angels descending from and ascending to heaven telling of that work which lay ahead for him in the future. Pilate's wife was warned in a dream that Jesus was an innocent, just person. Dreams are constant reminders as to what is happening in your life; look upon them as barometers. When your dreams improve, it is always a sign of soul progression.

Take time to remember your dreams for they are a storehouse of knowledge, wisdom and advice for your future. Nothing major or minor ever occurs in your life without your dreaming about it first. Keep a pen and paper at your bedside. Before falling asleep at night, after you have taken stock of your day's progress, after you have prayed, after you have meditated give yourself the suggestion to answer one question of importance to your soul's progression in a dream, and the suggestion that you will remember that dream the next morning. In the morning upon waking, sit at the edge of your bed, feet firmly placed on the floor, then try to remember as much as possible of your dream. Write it down and keep a daily dream diary. This requires discipline! The rewards will be great, for after several weeks, you shall see signs and proof of many future events. They will not be earth-shaking predictions unless you live an earth-shaking life. Why is this so important? Because of what dreams are. As music is the language of the world, so dreams are the language of soul. Symbols are often of great importance in this unusual language. Study your dreams and learn their meanings. Many of your problems can be solved more effectively if you begin to give rightful and due credit to dreams.

Your friends upon Earth-Eden can speak to you in dreams. Souls from the Second Realm can speak to you in dreams. Guides and teachers can speak to you from the Third Realm in dreams. Guardian angels and saints can speak to you from higher realms in dreams, and Infinite, Intelligent, Creative Love, can speak to you in dreams and you can reply in dreams.

Upon Earth-Eden today there are sophisticated sleep-testing laboratories in which much study is being made on a scientific level to understand dreams. This work is quite important, but equally so is your work! Discipline is the key word here. Once you have formed the habit of recording your dreams, you will find progression unlimited. Go over the steps mentioned earlier in this chapter, following each step as outlined. What have you to lose? Your dreams can help work out your problems. Remember the old saying, "let me sleep on it." The ancients were very advanced in harnessing the power of dreams and you can do likewise.

The following is a recorded transcript of my second session of speaking while in an enlightened state of consciousness:

"Infinite, Intelligent, Creative Love, I ask you to help me at this time as I attempt my second session of inspirational speaking. In this chapter dealing with "dreams," I ask for more information with which I may help others in their soul progression. I ask that my body and soul be protected while doing this work, and I ask blessings upon those who are helping in this communication. I ask this in the Spirit of Truth and in the name of the Master who is my Pathshower. Amen.

Clear the mind."

The mind is clear.

"Please answer all questions. Go to whom, to what, to where, in order to receive these answers in the Love of Infinite, Intelligence. Please tell me when you are ready."

We are ready.

Unto whom information is given, unto those who seek this information, guidance is the keynote, for misuse in the interpreting of dreams can be a deterrent on the path of progression. Interpretation is to be practiced only by those who have by small yet constant steps ascended to this talent. This ability needs development. The importance of interpreting dreams is for each person to understand that the language of the soul has no known vocabulary and is not limited with words and letters which even humans at times find wanting. Souls in higher realms need not dream; dreaming is basically a physical virtue and that is precisely what it is, a virtue, probably the last dormant one and that which is least observed. This virtue stands equally with mathematics and healing, for no pyramid could ever have been built without dreaming thereof first.

We would ask you to continue in one hour. Thank you, we are finished! Awaken protected and refreshed, awaken.

Here I must interrupt once more. You can't imagine my surprise at the abrupt ending of this last inspirational speaking session. You will be even more surprised when you read the second portion of it which I channeled exactly one hour later.

"Creative Love, once more I ask for Your guidance in receiving information on 'dreams' for the writing of this book. Since it was suggested one hour ago that there be a break, I therefore continue now. I ask for protection of my body and soul during this session. Amen."

"Clear the mind."

The mind is clear.

"Please answer all questions pertaining to 'dreams' for the writing of this chapter. Go to where, to what, to whom it is necessary to receive this information, staying constantly within the guidelines of Infinite, Intelligent, Creative Love. Please tell me when you are ready."

We are ready.

A reprimand is necessary at this point! Although it is only your second speaking session, you have not followed instructions properly. Yes, you were lying from north to south, but you were instructed not to do a session right after eating and, although we could have continued under that condition, you had some beer with your meal and the alcohol content is not what we need for these sessions. Please add this to your instructions that even though you drink a limited amount of alcohol, it, like food, is not to be taken at least one hour before any session. It would also be wise to add that you never do a session when tired, ill, angry or under medication. Let us pick up where we left off before!

No pyramid could ever have been built without one's dreaming thereof first. No healing can take place without one's thoroughly going through the entire dream-process beforehand. Although the dreams may not be remembered by the conscious, the subconscious certainly does so and records them.

Healing, be it of a mental or physical nature, is still healing, and both types are expressed in dreams before healing takes place. The recording mechanism of dreams is as what you would deem today a computer; but it would be as a computer of Creative Love precisely primed beforehand with all the details of a given situation, and one which mentally goes back and forth over the possibilities pro and con, for minuscule acts like baking a cake or grander resolutions like settling a family argument through Infinite Intelligence.

Souls in higher realms do not need dreams because there they are not in the physical and are closer to Creative Love. Since the human ego often needs curbing, often is tense, the information is given in dreams to counteract these situations. The dream weeds out the problems; it is the 'dry-run.'

Keep a pad and pencil next to your bed and, upon awakening, try to remember all or parts of your dreams. Many are understandable, but those dreams which you do not understand should still be recorded. You may not care to do this at an early hour, but it is best, for as time passes, your chances for recall are less. After a period of a month or two, go back over your notes or symbols and you will discover patterns. If you are wise enough to do this experiment, you are wise enough to grow in the interpretation of those dreams. But once more—patience, patience.

Many of the great literary works of history were dreamed, if not word for word, certainly first in concept. It was up to the authors to properly interpret, then to write the dreams whether or not the authors realized they were dreams. Any great structure which was ever built was dreamed first.

Dreams, the universal language of the soul, aid the individual even in nightmares. They are a release of emotions which need correcting. Those who say that they do not dream simply ignore remembering them, or their subconscious keeps it from them for a specific reason. However, it is generally best to understand your dreams, for much can be learned, and your personal spirit-guides can help make corrections and adjustments if you but let them; therefore, follow their advice, since they are in higher realms than you. Understand that the entire purpose of dreams is the communication of Infinite Intelligence to the soul.

We are finished. With love, with refreshment, awaken in obedience.

I wish each of you could have been here with me to experience this second session. I shall never forget it. I will continue this book through inspirational writing and perhaps one more inspirational speaking session near the end; however, remember that the source of the inspirational speaking sessions and the inspirational writing sessions is the same.

Chapter 13
Obedience Progression

"Listen to that still small voice" within *you* (1 Kings 19: 12); follow the intuition that is *yours*. Always look within where the answers for *your* lessons of life and the progression of *your* soul can be found.

The integrity, the dignity, the moral strength within each soul are the sparks of Creative Love which lighten the path of progression with constant unfoldment for each human being who strives to follow the spiritual callings rather than the physical lures.

Self-esteem is the beginning of co-esteem with Creative Love. As co-esteemers with Creative Love, you must also assume responsibility in the teaching and helping of less elevated souls. You must reflect Creative Love in concern for the spiritual welfare of your brothers and sisters as Creative Love constantly is concerned about *you* and *your* return. Think constructive thoughts, speak constructive words, do constructive deeds, thus re-creating and co-creating with Infinite, Intelligent, Creative Love desirable conditions upon Earth-Eden. The virtue of patience leads to the virtue of discipline which, in the staircase of small yet constant steps, ascends to the virtue of obedience! Obedience to the Law of Infinite Intelligence brings about Loving Peace. "Thy Will be done" (Matt. 6:10), taught the Master. The highest, greatest and final step of Creative Consciousness is to live within the Laws of Infinite Intelligence, to become at-one with it. The Atonement! This can be achieved by ridding oneself of fear (the lack of trust in Infinite Intelligence which has gotten humans into many an earthly mess)!

Repeat positive affirmations to yourself such as: "Since no one, or no thing is greater than Infinite, Intelligent, Creative, Love, and this kind, compassionate Love loves me so much as to have created me, whom or what shall I fear?" Realize your *oneness* with the whole of creation, not your separateness. All you need is constantly at your disposal from the Infinite Source if you but realize this *truth*! It's yours for the taking! "Your abundance-cup runneth over" (Ps. 23:5)! Once more, look towards your Pathshower and Example of Creative Consciousness, who came to live within the Law of Obedience! He meditated in Gethsemane for the Law to take that bitter cup from him, for he *did not* want to die in such a manner, but he also said: "Not My will, but Thine be done" (Mark 14:36). Obedient even unto death upon the cross. It was in this final giving-up-of-self that he attained the highest degree of Creative Consciousness of any human. He, in fact, became the Christ through obedience.

In the New Testament you can read of Jesus' struggle: "Who (Jesus) in the days of his flesh, when he offered up prayers and supplications with strong crying and tears unto Him (Principal Law) that was able to save him (Jesus) from death, and was heard in what he feared; though he was a son, yet learned obedience by the things which he suffered, and being made perfect (in Creative Consciousness), he became the author of eternal salvation (the Pathshower) unto all of them that obey Him, (Principal Law)" (Heb. 5:7-9). Follow the teachings, not like those who simply go to church every week, voicing prayers with which they often create more regression for themselves through hypocrisy by calling Jesus "the Messiah, the Redeemer, the Saviour," and then not living in obedience to these teachings. For which souls have more the heart of Creative Love, those who belong to overstructured religious organizations, yet are not obedient to Love's Ways in their daily actions and transactions, or those who do not take part in grand titles and rituals, but obey the Commandments of Infinite Intelligence? Remember, you are upon Earth-Eden for the progression of your soul and *nothing* else! Don't fool yourself! The Law will not be mocked! You have free will. You are the one who elevates or condemns yourself in your thoughts, words and deeds! Not Creative Love! It really is not that difficult to obey and begin to progress. Try it; it can become a habit.

Have confidence in your obedience, for in confidence is the

ever peaceful key which unlocks the binding chains of fear (lack of trust in Infinite Intelligence). This enables you to elevate your soul by small yet constant steps up the staircase of trust to the plateau of obedience which you now know to be the greatest gift which you can give to Creative Love. Everything else Creative Love has given to you, and in offering *other* gifts, you merely give back what was a gift; but obedience is truly a free gift which belongs entirely to you. By obeying Love's Principle, the Pathshower's teachings, and your own good conscience, you truly are giving up self!

Remember the unwritten eleventh commandment, "Thou shall not waste." In not obeying Creative Love, you are committing needless regression: the waste of time. As you have been told before, time is a valuable commodity upon Earth-Eden and, as the precious grains of sand slip through the hour-glass of years, your actions become more and more a pattern, a habit. If obedience is not a part of those patterns, those habits, do something about it *now*. Let us repeat what we have said earlier in this book—*"now is your day of salvation"* (2 Cor. 6:2)! *Now*! Today is great with opportunities for growth and for all that is good. Make use of these opportunities, for the sands of time flow steadily and wait for no one; lest you be as the five foolish maidens who brought no oil with their lamps and when the bridegroom came in the dark of night, they were not able to be with him (Matt. 25:1-13). Since few know when their hour for passing from Earth-Eden is to come, it is best to be prepared. Have the oil of obedience in your lamp of trust which lightens the darkness of your ignorance of Infinite Intelligence and prepares you for the wedding of your soul to Infinite Intelligence, and for your eternal home.

There are endless examples of obedience in the scriptures such as the prophets, the apostles, Joseph, Mary, and Jesus. Observe the obedience practiced by those last three entities. Joseph obeyed *every* request made of him in dreams. Every one! Mary obeyed when the angel appeared to her (Luke 1:38). She did not hesitate, she did not say no; she obeyed then and throughout her life. Jesus obeyed to the bitter end, *every time* placing Infinite Intelligence before self. At Cana's wedding feast, it was Mary, herself, who told the wine stewards to obey the Master (John 2:1-11) which resulted in his first so-called recorded miracle . Remember, it seems a miracle only to unenlightened human souls. For the more highly progressed souls, there are no miracles; rather, a fuller understanding of the endless power attained through obedience to Infinite Intelligence.

It was when the pallbearers of the widow's only son obeyed the Master and stopped their procession to the cemetery that He again demonstrated Creative Consciousness by bringing the soul of her son back into his physical body (a resurrection) (Luke 7:11-18). Understand that only after a soul has learned obedience to Love's Will can that soul proportionately demonstrate Creative Consciousness. Only through obedience can one end the wheel of Karma, enter Grace, and begin a faster journey to at-one-ment with ever-loving, ever-caring, mother-father, sister-brother, Creative Love. "At-one-ment" is "atonement" which is "attainment" of Creative Consciousness.

As earthly parents seek the obedience of their children for proper growth and progression, so it is with each living soul and Infinite Intelligence. When children are disobedient at home or school, it is wise for parents or teachers to lovingly discipline them according to the degree of their disobedience, in order for them to learn and understand correct behavior. This can take any of several forms of correction which may unfortunately seem to be punishment; but remember that sadly it is through suffering, restriction and disappointment that much progression is achieved. Infinite Intelligence does not punish you personally. You are constantly given the opportunity through the Law of Karma to correct your errors of cause and effect, or, through the highest Law of Grace, to learn the wrong of your errors by asking forgiveness and honestly trying to regress no more.

Obedience becomes less a task and more the preferred way of life if you look at it as a gift and privilege. For which would you choose, darkness or light, poorness in enlightenment or richness in soul progression, greed or altruism?

Chapter 14
Altruistic Progression

Altruism is the result of obedience. It is a word which is not frequently used upon Earth-Eden today and is found to be primarily in the hearts and minds of those souls who truly are sincere seekers on the path of soul progression. Buddhism, Christianity and some other religions are founded upon it, yet a very small percentage of either group lives it fully. But this is not to ignore that small percentage who do. There are "those among you" who are to be commended and followed, for their ways demonstrate more than those of others the enlightenment and pureness of Creative Love upon Earth-Eden. These are "angels of mercy" in higher stages of unfoldment who have taken on human bodies although they did not have to return to Earth-Eden; rather they chose to do so in order to help other souls reach Creative Consciousness.

Altruism is the *practice* of caring for the physical and spiritual welfare of others. There is the story of a certain young rich man who asked the Master what he must do in order to become one of his disciples, and the Master told him to sell all his material holdings and give the money to the poor. This was surely a noble request with a noble reply. As the story goes, the rich man turned sadly away and did not become a disciple for he had many great material riches and could not part with them. The Master looked into the man's soul, then read the Akashic records of his past incarnations, and saw that the main lesson which this young rich man had to learn in his then, present incarnation was to rid himself of greed, the opposite of altruism. He may have been a very friendly person, he may have been fun to be with, he may have been very handsome, but he did not wish to share his material wealth and that is all too often an outward sign of inner greed (Mark 10:17-27)!

Then there is the story of another rich man who had so much material wealth that he decided to tear down his barns and build larger ones which would hold his numerous possessions rather than giving of his material abundance to those less fortunate. You know his end, he died that night and had to meet self (Luke 12:13-21)!

These are merely examples lacking physical altruism. Now, let us take a look at vocal altruism. How rich many of you are with words. How often a kind word spoken will aid and comfort someone in distress and yet many a person rich with words remains greedily silent!

Last, but most certainly not least, is mental altruism, the altruism of greatest strength, the "building" altruism of thought. Think well of others, judge them not harshly, always give them the benefit of the doubt. Love your enemies, think well and pray for those who persecute and despitefully use you (Matt. 5:44). Turn the other cheek (Matt. 5:39). Judge not unjustly so that you will not be judged unjustly (Matt. 7:1-2). Condemn not the regressive soul, rather the regression, so that *you* will not be condemned. Do unto others as you would have others do unto *you* (Matt. 7:1). These are the teachings of the Creative Conscious Pathshower: be kind in thought, word, and deed thus progressing in soul. For such is the state of altruism. Would you want Creative Love to be any other way? Then treat others kindly and compassionately in your thoughts, for those thoughts will become words and those words will become deeds. Be careful, for as you think, so you are. Also, be altruistic with *yourself* in thought, word and deed. Do not think lowly of yourself, do not discredit yourself in words to others, and do not cheat yourself out of meeting your own necessary material and spiritual needs. For to go to such extremes is not being altruistic to yourself.

Altruism is kindness, compassion and concern for the welfare of others and yourself. Remember at the end of the first inspirational speaking session, we ended with: "*Me* is *I; I* is *I Am; I Am* is *Us;* and *Us* is *We.*" This is a very simplified explanation of your relationship with your own self, with others, with Creative Love, and Creative Love's relationship with all. These relationships are based on altruism, a concerning Love.

Altruism can also be called self-less-ness or ego-less-ness, for it is the pathway which leads to one of the higher principles of progression, namely that of the concern for and the help of others. Worry not about what those of lowly spiritual progression say. Be called the fool, be called the idiot for doing good, for was not even the Teacher of teachers "spat upon" (Matt. 26:67)? Names may hurt but they need not hinder your progression; rather, they can very well serve as a reversed energy (that energy wasted by regression) and aid you in your altruism. Not everyone will agree with your goodness, but you will be setting an example, you will be progressing and you will be helping *some* of the others.

Learn to think without the words "I," "me" and "mine." Learn to speak these words less frequently. Learn to become more active in deeds not concerning yourself. Then the "I" becomes aware of the *"I Am"* (Infinite Intelligence) and also becomes more aware of the "*Us*" and *"We"* (all souls and Creative Love). In order to achieve this altruistic mental progression, it is necessary to remove yourself from false friendships, unvirtuous acquaintances and irreverent places, therefore becoming unfettered from poor habits and lust. Rather, seek out those souls who demonstrate the level of progression to which you would like to elevate yourself. It will also be necessary to remove yourself physically from the location where you reside for periods of time. Take weekend retreats of isolation, read, pray and meditate. Take a hiatus in your life and relocate for a few weeks if possible to a place of serenity, beauty and quiet. There is much to be gained in altruistic mental progression, for it will lead to new horizons of greater enlightenment. In doing so, you become more in harmony with yourself and with others, thus awakening to the fact that you are in closer harmony with Creative Love: *I* to *Us*.

After you have begun this physical and mental change in your life, seek out a teacher who can help you further. Attend lectures of various religions, societies and organizations. Stay with your mentors until you have outgrown them or have found others to help you progress into a higher enlightenment. "Seek and you *shall* find, knock and it *shall* be opened to you" (Matt. 7:7) in your daily life both physically and spiritually.

Purchase books, visit libraries and place yourself on worthwhile mailing lists. There is an endless storehouse of wisdom at your fingertips which is yours for the taking, more than all the destroyed writings of the grand library of Alexandria (as we have told you in the chapter of Gem Progression) and more than all the buried scrolls upon Earth-Eden. As you read, as you learn, begin to write down progressive ideas; this is a sure sign of a soul's striving toward enlightenment. As you begin to write, concentrate upon the altruistic aspect of your writings which are lessons from your inner self to be followed. Read and re-read your lessons, for that still small voice within is purely altruistic in nature and is the purest part of you which is in direct communion with Creative Love, the source of your creative Spirit of Truth.

It is Love's basic characteristic to be concerned with the welfare of every soul which it created out of Infinite Intelligence. This means not only caring about the welfare and soul progression of your friends, but also caring for the welfare and soul progressions of your enemies. To do good to those who love you is no difficult task, but to do good to those who hate you is an immense progression for your soul. Remember, *all* souls were created by the same Intelligence with the same Love. The Nazarene said, "How can you say that you love God (Creative Love), whom you have not seen, yet love not your neighbor whom you have seen" (1 John 4:20)? Care about the soul progression of yourself and that of others. All are upon Earth-Eden for soul progression; some are of higher progression, some are of lower progression. The Nazarene also said, "The poor you shall always have with you" (Mark 14:7). The poor in spiritual ignorance, the poor in physical need. When the Teacher of teachers made that statement, he was not only prayerfully addressing the people of Israel in that day but all souls for all times to come. Since he saw much physical and spiritual poverty in their midst, he was trying to tell them that Creative Love loved them, physically poor as they were, and wished for them to elevate their souls to greater spiritual richness. The Teacher from Nazareth taught through altruism in his constant caring for their

1 welfare. This was the example which Creative Love wanted him to set, and prove to humans how much *can* be done. Care, care, care about others, for you certainly want Creative Love to care about you. This is being truly religious.

Chapter 15
Religious Progression

Religious progression is rare. Unfortunately, in many of its dealings throughout human history it has been religious regression. The overstructured religions that humans have conjured up since they first entered upon Earth-Eden have been greatly based upon error and untruth. Sadly, often whenever the soul of a master-teacher re-enters upon Earth-Eden for the length of a human life span in order to bring about enlightenment for enlightenment's sake, eventually, after the physical death of the flesh vessel of that master-teacher a religion develops. It then grows into an over-organized structure with endless rules, regulations, laws, rituals, creeds and ceremonies which soon drift far from the teacher's pure, original truth into political power, greed and often the complete opposite of Infinite Intelligence. We cannot emphasize enough that Earth-Eden does not need another overstructured religion. What is greatly needed is for all the various religions to purge themselves of hypocrisy and open their doors to constant reformation and enlightenment by granting equality to *all* of their members.

Unfortunately, some overstructured religions have created much corruption in the past fifteen thousand years (from Atlantis to the present) and their ways are not easy to stop. The words "true religion" have practically no meaning, because when spoken, humans think of organized associations. However, if we could convey to you any idea worth reasoning with pertaining to so-called religion, then we would repeat what many a master-teacher has already said to you upon Earth-Eden. A list of these would include famous names which we feel no need to repeat at this time with the exception of Moses, Ruth, Zoroaster, Buddha, Jesus and Origen. They simply taught that all people are to be treated equally regardless of what the human eye may see as their so-called differences. They truly understood God's Love.

Religion should be nothing else except what we have been telling you throughout this book, namely, kindness, compassion, honesty, justice, respect, equality and your will to progress to the point of Infinite Intelligence! Ultimately, Creative Love is all that is needed. If only you humans would trust in Infinite Intelligence and strive to return to its Principal Ways! *All* of you are sisters and brothers as children of Creative Love. You *are* your neighbor's keeper (keeping concern for their souls as Creative Love keeps concern for your soul) (Gen. 4:9). Feed the hungry, aid the poor, the afflicted, the homeless, the orphan, the aging, the lonely, the prisoner and the sick (Matt. 25:35-44). Visit and aid *personally*. For as we have asked you in the past, would you ever expect Creative Love to be any less compassionate with you, remembering all of your shortcomings?

Volumes could be written about what religion is not, but we are not interested in giving so much valuable time to negative deeds. We will mention but a few worthless, non-progressive actions which unfortunately too many accept on blind faith. Notice the word "faith" has seldom been used within these pages, for all too often it is grossly blind and does more harm than good. We have mainly used the words "trust" and "understanding" which are much more progressive. Nevertheless, here are some heavenly, soulful *facts* which religion is not:

Repetitive mumbled prayers, boringly recited at a pace which no human being can meditate upon.

Prayers which bargain with Infinite Intelligence.

Prayers which tell Infinite Intelligence how to run the universe.

Prayers which greedily ask for material wealth.

Prayers which want Infinite Intelligence to do your soul progression for you.

Songs with all the same negative nature as above which are falsely called "praise"!

Religions built on the chance of mammon, rather than on the understanding of Infinite Intelligence.

Religions which teach these chance ideas to their young and older members through raffles and games of gambling, rather than teaching Creative Love and creating an opportunity for the members to give lovingly, and teaching *trust* in Infinite Intelligence, for Creative Love has *never* gambled with you, has *never* failed you! Therefore, do not rely upon chance for your spiritual growth, just as you do not rely upon chance for your physical growth. As you work to earn your physical maintenance, so you must work to earn your spiritual maintenance. Trust in Infinite Intelligence, for "you shall not live on bread alone, but by every Word (Truth, Trust) which comes from the largess of God (Creative Love)" (Matt. 4:4). "In the beginning was the Word and the Word is God" (and shall continue to be Infinite, Intelligent, Creative Love) (John 1:1-2). Return to that Love.

The selling of candles for a profit. Creative Love does not need to be bribed by a tiny light. Teach the members that Infinite Intelligence *is* the Light Eternal, Eternal Enlightenment. Go out and reflect that light in thought, word and deed.

The selling of rituals in forms of prayers for the dead. *God for bid!!* Pray *yourself* from the bottom of your heart for your departed and teach others to do likewise.

Giving material and monetary gifts, with your name as donor engraved upon them. Who cares? *No one*, except you and your own ego (self)!

The preaching of sermons not lived by the preacher, who is seen by the members who follow and do likewise.

The building of gigantic edifices at immense costs while less fortunate souls are in physical and spiritual need, little relief from which they find in those edifices.

The wearing of expensive robes to adorn the body when the soul therein should be adorned in the simplicity of the Master's teachings and Creative Love.

Taking expensive vacation trips to so-called holy places sponsored by some overstructured religions while people of other religions are in need.

Rejecting other humans from positions within the so-called religion because of their age, gender, marital status, sexual orientation, creed or color (Imagine if Creative Love did *that*!).

Permitting killing on so-called religious moral grounds.

Cheating employees within the organization by not paying standard wages.

Teaching hatred toward other so-called religions, stating falsely that theirs is the only true religion.

Becoming a political power and lauding over the people rather than guiding them in soul progression.

We shall go no further for the picture is quite clear. Now, let us remind you that within every overstructured religion there are souls who *have* progressed within these structures, and there even are a few denominations within the vast religious structures that *do* practice a more advanced demonstration of soul progressiveness than many of the others. They may be few in number, but these advanced souls *can* teach the multitudes by *example*!

As we have said before, another overstructured religion is not needed. Many highly progressed souls, "those among you" who have entered upon Earth-Eden, have accomplished great works of enlightenment without overstructure because they worked through Creative Consciousness as did the Galilean Teacher. He *never* intended the tight overstructure which led to the "crusades" and the "inquisition." He taught of the individual living temple which each of you are.

The church was not founded upon Peter, "the rock," for when Jesus was taken away, Peter denied him three times, and the rock of Peter crumbled into the sandstone of fear-dust. Rather, the church *is* founded upon the sure foundation of the cornerstone of the Nazarene as he demonstrated Creative Consciousness, as the Example, the Pathshower, the Redeemer. That Essene Jew from Nazareth taught a simple way. He most certainly believed in simplicity and trust in Creative Love for his physical and spiritual life. He rebuffed the Sanhedrin who ran the overstructured temple in Jerusalem and would do the same with leaders of the overstructured, ritualistic religions of today. He was a person who deflated pompous egos, many of whom are still found in the hierarchy today. He would cherish many monks and nuns of the various religions, for often they truly live a simple and serving life, traveling along the straight, narrow and upward path.

It isn't that organized religion is entirely wrong or entirely unnecessary, but *over*-structure is overstructure and robs one of valuable time; also, needless rituals are often followed more than the tenets of the Master. As the Master is Simplicity, so is Simplicity the Master. In the temples and churches today there is a constant need for simplicity and the understanding of proper teachings, plus the witness of those lessons in demonstration. There is much for many to learn in the various institutions, and there is also much for many of the various institutions to learn.

"Seek and you shall find" (Matt. 7:7), taught the Master Teacher and so it is also with some overstructured religions. Seek out the one which is best suited for your needs and your present progression. When it no longer fulfills your needs, speak to those in charge and the members of the congregation to see how you and they can begin to elevate unfoldment in soul progression, but take heed, for it is more than likely that you will find strong stubbornness and opposition. Try your best, always remembering that after several soulful tries within a fairly substantial period of time, after much meditation and Creative Demonstration in thought, word and deed, if they do not elevate or progress, find a better organization or do without. Eventually you will make faster progress with the ability to help others through your example, and this can be achieved by your not playing a martyr role. If, however, they will not progress, leave the headstrong entities to their own lot, stomp the dust of their stubbornness from your shoes and continue elsewhere with your life in demonstrating Creative Consciousness, for that is truly what religion should be. Buildings are not the church; the church is Creative Consciousness demonstrated by you.

Some organized churches of various denominations truly teach and follow the lessons of the Master on a higher level than others; unfortunately, many also show poor manners to churches of other denominations even to the point of calling some non-Christian. Sadly, many church members do not place the idea of soul progression high on their priority list of life's achievements. Life should be your religion and religion should be your life. Meditate, live properly and honestly; for money, wealth, position, beauty and fame are like the chaff which the wind driveth away (Ps. 1:4). You take none of those things with you when you pass through the change called death. Infinite Principle is no respecter of age, gender, marital status, sexual orientation, race or religion; rather, Infinite Principle is a respecter of hearts. When Creative Love looks into your heart, what will be found there?

Too many churches teach that if you believe in Christ you are "saved" and will go to Heaven when you die, and some churches even teach that after living a terrible life, upon your deathbed you can ask for forgiveness and all is wonderful and forgotten! That is *not* the way it is, my friends. A soul who has led a terrible life does not reform in the twinkling of an eye, for it has taken that soul years of regression to do so, if not several incarnations! Fear at the time of death does not necessarily bring about trust in Infinite Intelligence or total sorrow if one lived a terrible life, and even if in rare cases it does, the soul would have forgiveness (for Creative Love always forgives), but it does not mean that one must not make up for all of one's wrongs. *That always* takes time! Forgiveness *needs* its partner of contrition!

Another wrong teaching of many churches is what happens to an entity's soul when the body dies. In Creative Love's house are many mansions and a place is prepared for *all* according to their soul progression (deeds or lack of deeds) (John 14:2). It's not a rose garden for everyone when the silver cord is severed and they enter into the next realm, just as it is not a rose garden for everyone when the umbilical cord is severed and they enter upon the First Realm of Earth-Eden (Eccl. 12:6).

Concerning those of low soul progression or those who truly with blind faith believed in false teachings, it is often a difficult task for their guides and administering angels to convince them that they have passed over and are no longer in the physical body. Remember, mind is ever the builder upon Earth-Eden and is so even after the change called death. However, those souls of high soul progression or those who rejected blind faith and false teachings, who sought mentally to find higher spiritual counseling and proof of life after the change called death, are in a much finer state of mind after passing over. They understand, accept and progress in soul much faster. They recognize their loved ones who have passed over before them who are there to greet them. These progressed souls are much happier and spiritually healthier than others who have not been taught the truth.

There are temples of learning in that next realm (the Second Realm which is very close to Earth-Eden, in a manner of speaking) in which Creative Consciousness is taught, demonstrated and learned. There is also heartfelt grief there because of false teachings upon Earth-Eden concerning what happens after the change called death. For example: a man in his mid-fifties who has no belief in the afterlife dies suddenly in an auto crash. In the twinkling of an eye, he is quickly swept out of the physical body and simply does not understand what has happened to him. His spirit floats near his dead body and tries relentlessly to re-enter it. When guides arrive to help him, he does not see them for his thoughts are of such physical understanding that he simply rejects the idea that he has passed. When loved ones who have passed beyond are brought to him, he reacts toward them in the same way. It could be months, if not years, before he is no longer earthbound and can progress in spirit.

Another example: a ten year old girl who, after a long illness, finally passes over. Because she was wrongly taught by overstructured religion, she refuses to believe the ministering angels when they present the child's passed grandparents to her and all are heartbroken. She had been taught that after death a soul goes to a heaven of clouds to be met by Jesus, God, or a hell of flames with Lucifer or devils. She thinks that she is still upon Earth-Eden and cries, wanting to be returned to her parents. Many of those who have passed over, as well as guides and ministering angels, pray for proper teaching upon Earth-Eden in dire anguish, wishing for their tasks to be joyous rather than nightmares.

Thanks be to those advanced souls who lovingly minister in these severe circumstances and who continue to teach, help and comfort those unenlightened souls when they pass over. We will continue along these thoughts in the next chapter, dealing more fully with the change called death.

Chapter 16
Death Progression

An entity which has become unconscious or may have just died can often still hear; therefore, beware what you say, for hearing is one of the last physical senses of the body to cease. In most cases, death is not a fast process. Death, like birth, concerns the will of an immortal living soul about to leave or enter the flesh and often it is not a decision easily made!

When the time of passing is near, the soul of that entity may hover between two worlds, whether in the body or outside near the body (similar to the re-entry process of birth), and often in that conscious, semi-conscious, or even seemingly unconscious state, the person may still hear and see those in the flesh who are near, and also hear and see those in the spirit who are near. The person may see so-called "dead" relatives or friends and try to talk with them and may actually hear what they say. Those on the spiritual side of life, be they guides, friends, relatives or angels, may either ask the dying entity's soul to let go and follow them, or they may advise the person to fight for life in the flesh and to continue that incarnation for the special purpose which had been chosen but which has not yet been accomplished.

The same power and opportunity is given to you who are still in the flesh. You too may advise a soul near death to "let go" (if the physical body is very old with a sever illness;) or you may advise it not to die (if the physical body is very young and reasonably healthy), and to return to its body with the understanding that Creative Love will guide it in this incarnation to finish the task it has chosen upon Earth-Eden. That is the same Creative Consciousness which the Master demonstrated when he resurrected others. He taught you to follow his ways and said, "Even greater works than I, can you do" (John 14:12), if you but work, grow and progress soulfully by putting aside fear and gain trust in Creative Love through Creative Consciousness.

When individuals seem to be passing over and you feel that they should *die* because of their age or illness, instruct them gently, yet authoritatively with love, that they should let go. Tell them to follow the light, to have no fear, and to go with their spiritual loved ones whom they can now see and hear. Speak in this manner for at least a quarter-hour if possible, and *remove* from the room any who do not understand or do not agree.

When individuals seem to be passing over and you feel that they should *not* die because they are young, healthy or have much to live for, instruct them gently, yet authoritatively and with love, that they should fight for physical life. Tell them to stay in or re-enter the body, to have no fear, and to stay with their loved ones upon Earth-Eden whom they can still see and hear. Continue telling them of their life's task which they must complete (with Creative Love's help and yours). Speak in this manner for at least a quarter-hour if possible, and *remove* from the room any who do not understand or do not agree.

This is how the Master resurrected the daughter of Jairus, ruler of the synagogue (Mark 5:22-24, 35-42), the widow's son (Luke 7:11-17), and Lazarus (John 11:1-46). However, when advising a soul to remain in the flesh or to pass through death, be very sure of your motivation, be sure that the physical body is in good enough condition to house a soul for progression, for if you are not completely certain, do *not* do anything. This is a task only for a soul of advanced spiritual understanding, and being a member of the clergy does not necessarily give one the credentials for such a task. We repeat, it is a task only for a soul of advanced spiritual understanding who *lives* the Creative Consciousness.

The desire to have a loved one live as long as possible in the flesh is understandable, but do not allow selfish desire to cloud your motives or prevent your remembering our Master's promise of the survival of the soul after the death of the body. Love spans the gulf of the grave and continues in the world of spirit (and in other incarnations if that is to be the case). Do not aggrandize the flesh; for when the body has served its purpose, the soul must leave it in order to seek progression within the tranquility of the spirit world, or eventually to reincarnate again and work off Karma if it has not yet entered Grace through Creative Consciousness.

Death has been that feared yet often desired mystery which humans have been interested in since the race began. Although the various religions have tried to shed light on the subject, often the original truth of their founders was lost once the religion began to grow into an overstructured organization with rituals, creeds and laws. However, the Truth has always stayed the Truth, for until a soul has progressed through kindness, compassion, honesty, justice, respect, and equality (entering Grace), it continues to reincarnate until its dross of selfishness is burned off in a furnace of love and becomes goldenly pure in Creative Consciousness, desiring the flesh no more (Wisdom 3:5-6).

Realize that since there are no accidents in Infinite Intelligence (simply self meeting self), so is it also with much sickness. Surely Creative Love wishes none ill!! As the Master told, sickness often is simply a result of sin (self, selfishness, greed)! He asked "Is it easier to say 'arise and walk,' or 'your sins are forgiven'?" (Matt. 9:5).

Realize that you can overcome much sickness, but first you must, by small yet constant steps, weed out past wrongs committed by you to others or committed by others to you.

Realize that it is because of so-called human justice that there is a third world! Humans doing unto humans, self meeting self, yet Grace is constantly available; simply accept that Truth and start living your life in that manner.

Realize that there is no end to your existence, not even when the change called death takes place. And when the change called death does occur, your soul leaves the body and is eventually given its full memory. The personality of the last incarnation has become a part of your soul as have the personalities of all your previous incarnations. Then comes the time of judgment, but by whom? God? Not really. You have already judged yourself in the very acts of right and wrong which you have committed or have not committed, and depending upon how far your soul has advanced, you could be in line for several situations:

If you have advanced to the highest degree, you will no longer need to reincarnate, and there will be many other choices available to you at that point.

If you have advanced greatly, but not to the highest degree, you may stay a period of time for further advancement in the Spirit-Matter Realm (Second Realm) which is very close to Earth-Eden, then reincarnate by choice with council from various advanced souls.

If you have advanced little, you will be held in the Spirit-Matter Realm (Second Realm) under guidance for a required period of time, and will be helped to reincarnate eventually into a life-situation which hopefully will teach you better advancement.

If you have regressed somewhat, you will be held in the Spirit-Matter Realm (Second Realm) under stronger guidance and for a much longer period of time until a just reincarnation.

If you have regressed severely, you will be held within the Spirit-Matter Realm (Second Realm) for an endless period of time, with opportunity to be helped, or you will be reincarnated into what may seem to the unwise as a severe condition of life. You may return mentally or physically handicapped, be placed in an extremely low state of society or any of an endless number of situations which would cause the unknowing to ask "Why did God do this?" But as you can see, such is not the case. "That which was sown will be reaped" (Gal. 6:7). It would be cruel if there were no guiding, loving second, tenth or seventy-times-seventy (endless) chance. The door of reformation is never closed to the entering of Grace!

You must not fail to realize that it was humanity itself which created so-called death, for eons ago, in the beginning, before the souls which today inhabit human bodies and constantly reincarnate, all souls were with Infinite, Intelligent, Creative Love! It was the ego, the self, the selfishness, the greed, the lack of trust of foolish souls in Creative Love which caused many souls to enter the flesh and reincarnate; thus so-called birth, thus so-called death. It is the seekers of Light, Truth and Oneness with Principal, the souls who have themselves become elevated and enlightened to the point of wanting to return, who are the spiritually advanced souls. They will have accomplished their heavenly goal (rather than earthly desires) and end the cycle of reincarnation when they finally rise above the limited law of Karma through realizing their wrongs, realizing their regressions, realizing their greed, and then living in a Love-like manner as much as possible, in proportion to the degree to which they let go of matter. Then they will enter into the Principle Law of Loving Grace, having to die no more!

The 23rd Psalm, perhaps the most known of all songs attributed to David, has endless meanings of advancement for everyone who reads, studies, prays and lives it. He wrote in the 23rd Psalm the phrase "Yea, though I walk through the valley of the shadow of death, I shall fear no evil for Thou art with me." "*Shadow!*" He did not write "Yea, though I walk into the valley of death," but "*through* the valley of the *shadow*!" A shadow is the absence of light! This is all that human death is, an absence of understanding, the passing through a mist of unsureness, but then comes the morning with yesterday's sorrows behind.

If a soul is advanced enough, has risen above self, selfishness, greed, material need, sexual and political lust, through Creative Consciousness, it will return home through Grace rather than taking another spin around the wheel of needless Karma re-entering upon Earth-Eden again. Learn this lesson now!

Oh, you who dwell upon Earth-Eden, realize that it was not the intention of Infinite Intelligence for humans to dwell as you do upon Earth-Eden, to deface it, to destroy it! Earth *was to be* Eden!! Earth *was to be* the garden; it was where the lamb *was* to lie down next to the lion! But it is because of restless souls (*many of you are among these rebels!!!*) and Creative Love's constant, patient concern for your return that Infinite Intelligence turned the Garden of Paradise into a School of Constant Opportunity for Reformation. Earth-Eden was intended for a greater purpose and shall return to its original purpose someday. It is to be a peaceful paradise where the most advanced souls are to meet periodically with Infinite Intelligence!

Earth-Eden in its present condition is *not* your goal, Earth-Eden is not your home; but since you are there presently through "squatters rights," take advantage of the constant opportunities still given to you in order to enable you to advance sufficiently to return home. *Realize that not all* souls were disobedient! The majority stayed with Creative Love. Most of you who are in the flesh are not of the "ninety and nine," but rather of the one-one-hundredth whom the Good Shepherd constantly wishes to bring back safely into the fold (Matt. 18:12-14). The Good Shepherd *is* the Good Shepherd and Loves *all* who belong to the Good Shepherd, Who is constantly present and not as the hireling shepherd, who runs away when the wolf of evil, the wolf of fear, the wolf of false pride, comes along (John 10:14).

"Oh death, where is your sting? Oh grave, where is your victory" (1 Cor. 15:55)? There need not be a "sting" in the change called death, but unfortunately for many a poor soul who has been wrongly taught by various overstructured religions upon Earth-Eden, the traditional heaven, hell or purgatory which was expected has not been found. Many do not even realize that they have died because they have been confused by these wrong teachings. The victory of the grave certainly can be there for each and every one of you if you but do something about it *now*! Follow the Ten Commandments (Exod. 20:1-17), follow the Son of Bethlehem's commandment to love one another (John 15:12,17). Follow the path which he trod as he became more and more Creatively Conscious. Follow this additional commandment, "Thou shall not waste." Be it food, energy, talent, or time, waste is waste. It is not progressive.

Understand Earth-Eden as the First Realm, and the Second Realm (or Spirit-Matter Realm) as the place where souls go after the change called death occurs. It is very similar to earthly surroundings yet not a completely spiritual nor completely physical state. Although souls there do not have physical bodies, they have similar bodies called "astral" bodies. Both male and female still exist for a time in appearance but not in function as known on Earth-Eden. It is in this Second Realm where the soul's past and future progression is discussed. There are many realms; in Creative Love's house are many mansions (John 14:2).

The Third Realm (a purely spiritual realm) is for souls who no longer have need of matter. They shed the astral body and acquire what may best be described as a spiritual body (which is still a type of form) in preparation for further progression towards the Fourth Realm and beyond. The inspirational thoughts given to Curt through these inspirational writings came mainly from the Third Realm at this time. It is the realm of "Going Home." Scripture mentions Paul "caught up into the Third Heaven" (2 Cor. 12:2) and many have heard of being in "Seventh Heaven."

There are various realms. The important fact to remember is that the material for this book is not coming from the Second Realm but rather from the Third Realm and higher. Most books channeled from the Second Realm still use earthly names of souls who have passed over and are between incarnations. The Third Realm is a higher realm pleading like "a voice crying in the wilderness" (Matt. 3:3). Awake you souls upon Earth-Eden, for Creative Love loves you! For your own sakes, *awaken* from your spiritual slumbering and realize that you need not be reincarnated but can progress from your own love to Creative Love.

Interpret some of the old hymns which to the unwisely educated may seem trite. Put aside mode and have your soul listen to the angel voices' teachings. Your task in life is to help others more dearly every day. Prepare to experience continued existence after the change called death, in the blessed by-and-by where you will meet friends and

1 loved ones again in a more beautiful land. Therefore, praise all you souls the Love of Heaven and to Creative Love's Will your goals bring. If you but accept and progress in these facts and enter Grace, you shall die no more and shall no longer have need of a physical body.

Chapter 17
Body Progression

The resurrected body of the Pathshower Jesus was a re-formation (reformation) of the energy created by his reaching perfection in Creative Consciousness, thus changing the corruptible body into the incorruptible body or changing physical energy into spiritual energy as did his soul-mate mother when she left Earth-Eden, as well as did others (some of "those among you").

Jesus did *not* spend three days in the tomb. It was only about thirty-six hours from Friday afternoon when he died (Mark 15:42) until very early Sunday morning (Matt. 28:1) when the faithful women disciples found the empty tomb. Jesus' soul left the body on Friday afternoon (at which time he met with Archangel Gabriel and other angels of the Transition Band), and then, having reached perfection, re-entered the *glorified* body early Sunday morning. This Transition Band of Angels had been with him for quite some time before he was crucified. One of these angels was seen by the astonished women on Easter morning at the tomb when they were told that the Master had risen from death (Mark 16:5), and another two of these angels were seen several weeks later as they spoke to the apostles immediately after he had ascended from Earth-Eden (Acts 1:9-11).

Upon the Master's return into a body, there was instantly a tremendous burst of cosmic-spiritual energy which caused the quaking earth to help an angel roll away the stone which had sealed the tomb (Matt. 28:2). The physical body was changed into dust as the newly-glorified, reformed, incorruptible, spiritual, soul-body began to rise through and beyond the material walls of the sepulcher. He conquered matter, leaving the linen embalming shroud lying flat in perfect order with an imprint of the once-flesh vessel which He had inhabited while upon Earth-Eden.

The soul of the Teacher of teachers had reached the highest point of Creative Consciousness or the Spirit of Pure Holiness and transformed the physical body into a pure, perfected soul-body beyond the flesh, beyond the physical. This is why Jesus was called the Christ. That Highest of Souls could "appear" at various times to various people, and also in a room behind locked doors (John 20:19). He seemed to mortal eyes to be in the flesh, although he was no longer in the flesh and would soon ascend in the same manner (disappear) beyond human sight and understanding until such time when a return will be made in what many think of as the "second coming." At that time he shall again only "appear" as flesh and blood, since he has overcome the flesh needing to reincarnate no more. The soul of the Master will not be reincarnated again, will not need to enter the flesh again; rather, it will return after several thousand years of dwelling in at-one-ment with Infinite, Intelligent, Creative Love in the state of pure Spirit and will be seen face to face by many who have striven for soul progression by giving up self.

Those enlightened souls who are in the flesh at that time shall be the raptured (1 Thes. 4:17). They will not need to die of the flesh; rather, their flesh will die of its limited existence and they shall be re-formed through Creative Consciousness and rise above the physical to the at-one-ment with Infinite Intelligence. The hour is known by none in the flesh. Prepare now, for *now* is your day of salvation (2 Cor. 6:2). Change your concepts, change your non-progressive ways to soul progressive ways of kindness, compassion, honesty, justice, respect, and equality.

Now let us explain the earlier physical resurrections which the Master performed through Creative Consciousness. Those bodies which he raised from the dead were not bodies which were buried for long periods of time, for bodies which have decayed do *not* rise again.

The reason he could raise those bodies mentioned in the New Testament, as did Elijah in the Old Testament, and others since then in modern times, is that they were not dead for long periods of time. The souls of those entities were simply recalled inasmuch as they were still earthbound. They then returned to their bodies (resurrected) because their bodies were still in sufficiently good physical condition to sustain them; otherwise, a new body (reincarnation) would have been needed for a soul's re-entry upon Earth-Eden. The resurrections were accomplished because of the Master's and Elijah's high soul development in Creative Consciousness. Reincarnations, however, are accomplished because of each individual soul's desire to re-enter upon Earth-Eden in order to complete a task, work off Karma and gain soul progression.

Those resurrected bodies could in the present be termed "clinically dead" where the silver cord has not yet been severed (Eccl. 12:6). Bodies, however, which have been severely, physically injured, or had their nervous systems damaged through shock or drugs, can become soul-less. There are soul-less bodies in which the flesh is being kept alive through human, artificial mechanism, thus preventing the bodies from decaying, but unfortunately with the bodies not functioning properly enough to house souls with which to gain soul progression (the only reason for human life upon Earth-Eden)!

Some of these worthless flesh-vessels can be compared with false hope to broken wine bottles as if they might still contain the grape's nectar. In some cases where a person has been in a coma for many years and the body has been reduced to a vegetable, the soul also leaves the body but does *not* enter into another higher spiritual realm; rather, it is sadly tethered or earth-bound and hovers near the body though not necessarily in it. *Beware of what you are doing in the name of science upon Earth-Eden!!!* This is similarly the case in a soul's entry through physical birth; a soul can enter as early as conception, or in extreme situations hovers near the mother of the fetus a few hours before birth or even a few hours after the birth of the baby before entering that new flesh-vessel. For some, it is not an easy Karma which lies ahead in various specific reincarnations and often the soul has doubts and does not enter until it feels ready, or does not enter, and either another soul enters or the baby dies.

There is also the opportunity for the soul of any body to leave for a few hours. This can happen during an operation when the body is artificially made unconscious or if the body unexpectedly has had a great physical shock such as falling from a building, being hit by an automobile or being trapped in a burning building. In these instances, the soul can leave the body to avoid tremendous pain which it feels it may not be able to endure or which may cause death. The soul may not wish nor be permitted to die and leave Earth-Eden at that specific time because it may still be working off a specific Karma.

When there is a definite need for a soul's progression, it can also leave during the time when the body is asleep (out-of-the-body experience), to travel to another realm or another place upon Earth-Eden in order to learn more for its own progression or to assist a loved one. However, whenever the soul leaves temporarily, it always stays attached to the body by what may be called the "silver cord" (Eccl. 12:6) (we will explain this in greater detail later in this chapter) through which the mind (which is the "will" of the soul) is still able to command the brain (which is the "controlling organ" of the physical body). Never confuse the mind with the brain, for it is the mind which remembers all your past incarnations and gives forth that information to the brain only when necessary in either the conscious, semi-conscious, subconscious or the unconscious state.

It is also the mind's function to send simultaneous accounts of *every* minute detail of the entity's thoughts, words and deeds to the Third and Fourth Realms. There, *everything is eternally* recorded in the Akashic records from which every soul can learn progression by eventually meeting self, either while in the physical body through an "out-of-the-body-experience," or after the change called the death of the last reincarnation. *Every* soul reviews that last incarnation in comparison with all its other incarnations.

As humans reach the possibility of physical brain transplants, many of you will be quite surprised that the brain taken from a donor and given to a recipient, will *not* have the donor's memory as a rule, for the memory is that of the mind which stays with the soul. The body is only the temporary house of the soul and not the other way around. The donor's brain would simply begin to express the thoughts of the mind of the recipient if the physical body does not reject the foreign brain for any number of reasons, or if the soul of the donor does not become greedy and try to "possess" the body of the recipient! *Beware* of organ transplant misuse!! You have *not* yet co-created that well!!!

We wish to give all of you a severe warning concerning your physical organ transplants! Remember, the flesh is not your goal, all flesh eventually must die. You are to strive for an *end* to your reincarnations. Remember, you are all souls whose only purpose is to become more spiritual, *not* more physical. When you humans upon Earth-Eden begin to transplant animal organs into your own bodies, or even non-living organs, you are little by little straying spiritually and physically from the true purpose of your being. *Do not* become more animalistic, more artificial, for you do not want to regress as did a race during the Atlantean era when some humans were almost soul-less creatures, grotesque in nature and in being, created by other humans as serfs, slaves or humanoids. *Beware* of your intentions, for even those who were resurrected by Jesus eventually did have to die of the flesh and their physical bodies did *not* rise again. Now, we are *not* telling you not to have corrective surgery when it is needed to help you live a more comfortable and painless existence in order to complete the task of an incarnation, but we *are* saying that there is a proper time to pass from the flesh and that when this time arrives for each of you, not to prolong it artificially. *Beware* of your motives and *trust* in Infinite Intelligence.

The allotted time for a human incarnation can be much longer than it is presently, for eons ago it was much longer. Longevity can be attained individually only through proper, healthy, clean, physical and spiritual living, and then slowly from individuals to nations or all of Earth-Eden. However, you must have a reason for a longer stay in the physical and it must be for your and others' soul progression. It is of no value just to keep breathing and become a vegetable as are thousands in your so-called "homes" (perish the thought).

If you pay careful attention, you will notice that at times you can remember re-entering your present body after an "out-of-the-body experience" which you have had while asleep. You re-enter through the solar-plexus in a split second and often awake with a startled jerk which is simply a reaction of the nervous system. This happens when the sleeping body has been disturbed by a noise or the presence of another person, causing the out-of-the-body soul to re-enter immediately. However, even when the soul is out of the body, it still keeps contact through the silver cord.

Reference to the silver cord can be found in the book of Ecclesiastes, 12:6-7: "Whenever the silver cord is loosened, then shall the dust (the clay vessel of the body of flesh) return to the earth as it was; and the spirit (soul) shall return to God who gave it." The silver cord is a connecting cord from the soul to the body. It is this cable which supplies the body with spiritual and mental energy. It is entirely elastic, can reach endless destinations into the ether and consists of a substance which is almost pure spiritual energy.

The parapsychological terminology for this semi-substance is "ectoplasm." It connects the solar-plexus of the physical body to what may best be termed the solar-plexus of the astral body which is the vehicle of the soul while it is out of the physical body. It is this same substance of ectoplasm which formed the spiritual body of Samuel when he was summoned by the medium of Endor because of Saul's command (Old Testament) (1 Sam. 28:7), and the bodies of Moses and Elijah when they materialized to Jesus in what is known as the transfiguration (New Testament) (Mark 9:2-4). Its consistency is lighter than air. At times it can be seen at the moment of death as the soul leaves the body when the silver cord severs and gathers in a thin silver mist, which often hovers near the body for a few seconds and then vanishes from human sight as it continues on to the next realm. It actually has physical weight which will vary with each individual astral body as does the weight of each individual physical body. If the physical body were weighed before and after death, there would show a loss of several ounces in addition to the loss of the body's breath and fluids. It is the same substance that so-called ghosts or spirits are made of, which upon rare occasions may be seen by certain human eyes.

There are also rare times when a body may have two or more silver cords, naturally meaning two or more souls in one body. The reason for this is threefold.

First: As when a person is a medium, a psychic or a sensitive, and conducts regular sessions at various intervals in their Earth-Eden life, to do service for others in the way of soul progression such as writing a book in this manner through inspirational speaking and writing while in an enlightened state of consciousness. The second silver cord is temporarily attached to the psychic's body from the realm from which the information is being given by one or more higher advanced souls.

Second: as when in *extremely* rare cases lasting only a few minutes as a soul leaves its body permanently to let another soul enter in until the end of that body's physical life. This is what best may be termed "transcarnation." Transcarnation is exceedingly rare because of its exceedingly rare purpose. There are highly developed souls which enter the flesh to be upon Earth-Eden for special missions in order to teach humans Creative Love and help them to return from where they came; these are known as "those among you." They can be souls which have reincarnated many times and have gained high soul progression, or can be highly developed souls which have never been in the flesh. If their missions take longer than one earthly lifetime, and it is not wise for an uncompleted mission to end, that soul may die of its body and be permitted to enter another soul's younger body in order to continue its mission. This is *only* done with permission of the donor's soul, and permission is granted while the donor's body is asleep or in some other altered state of consciousness. It may be that the younger person, although having a good physical body, was not developing properly in soul progression it its present incarnation, and wished to save its soul from regression due to the desires of the flesh, alcohol, drugs, crime, gambling and such. The wise Master Guides on the spirit side of life then negotiate this situation and a transfer of souls in a living physical body is made. The soul who receives this body is almost always one who either lives alone, in a cloister, or is removed from society. As we have said earlier, this occurs in exceedingly rare instances for exceedingly rare missions.

Third: As when one or more spirits from the Second Realm take refuge in one body, with the result known as "possession." Yes, unfortunately, this is possible. In such cases there are several silver cords attached to one body. Jesus exorcised greedy earth-bound spirits (possessing souls) from a person whom history called "Legion" (meaning "many") (Mark 5:9). Through Creative Consciousness he forced them out of that body which they had possessed, and they in turn entered the flesh of a nearby herd of pigs which immediately ran off a cliff to drown in the sea below, leaving the soulfully ill spirits without a flesh vessel. The possessed person was then cured and the possessing souls were exorcised.

Those whom you term insane are often weak souls who are possessed by evil, earthbound souls or simply lost and confused earthbound souls who wish to remain upon Earth-Eden, and do so by overpowering a spiritually weak individual. *Do not try to be an exorcist if you do not know what you are doing!!* (We will explain exorcism in greater detail later in this chapter.) The scriptures warn not to play mediumistic games. Therefore when not properly trained, "Know thy spirit." We might quickly add, know yourself and your earthly acquaintances as well. *Do not* trust your soul progression to those who do not demonstrate Creative Consciousness in thought, word and deed. Do not play foolishly with the ouija board, automatic writing, seances, hypnotism or similar mental sessions unless you are guided through proper steps by a wise and concerned mentor. Remember, your body is not only the vessel which houses your soul, it is your Holy of Holies, your temple wherein Creative Love meets with you.

Be careful, be meditative and realize that Creative Love is Infinite Intelligence; the source of *all* your strength. Trust in it, for it never misleads you. Unfortunately through fear, weak souls of both Earth-Eden and the Second Realm at times fail in their trust. Remember that although you *all* have guardian angels who have chosen to help your souls progress, you are created with free will and are ever free agents concerning your destinies. You know your weaknesses. However, remember that Infinite Intelligence has supplied you with all necessary strength; therefore, by small yet constant steps elevate yourself spiritually.

We must also remind you that when a little child is possessed, its soul is not a little child. It is a soul which probably has reincarnated many times upon Earth-Eden, and may have been related to or acquainted with the possessing spirit or spirits causing double or multiple spirit entries in the body of one physical child. It is necessary to find a *proper* person to perform the dispossession or exorcism. Dispossession is not an easy or pleasant task, for as you are aware of difficult situations connected with having an unlawful tenant removed from a house, apartment or hotel room, therefore you may understand the difficulty with a case of possession.

The first step to be taken is the realization through Creative Consciousness that *both the victim and the possessor are souls which have been created by the same Love!* This exorcism must not be attempted merely on a level of professed faith, but on the secure foundation of pure Truth and understanding of Creative Consciousness. The mentor exorcist must then try in heart, mind and soul to cast out the possessing and to guide the souls of *both* victim and possessor toward their proper future paths of Creative Love. The mentor-exorcist also must keep in mind constantly that *both the victim and the possessor are souls which have been created by the same Love!* Jesus performed exorcisms by demonstrating Creative Consciousness. A member of the clergy does not necessarily have the appropriate credentials. Exorcism is a task for a secure, knowing, loving, caring, mentor, not for a wimp or a pompous ass!

The second step to be taken is for the mentor-exorcist to remove all weak or opposed individuals from the room and close the doors behind them. Then the mentor-exorcist must *silently* affirm the mentor-exorcist's trust in Infinite Intelligence and we repeat that it is a must that the mentor-exorcist constantly keeps in mind that *both the victim and the possessor are souls which have been created by the same Love!*

The mentor-exorcist must speak first to the victim (who may or may not respond), reassuring the victim that the help at hand to correct this situation is from Creative Love. Next, the mentor-exorcist must assure the possessor of the same help from the same source. The mentor-exorcist must be prepared for vile, verbal rebuke from the possessing soul speaking through the mouth of the victim. The mentor-exorcist *must* command it to be silent and *must* reaffirm the mentor-exorcist's own thoughts instantly if they momentarily stray. It *always* helps to call forward any souls from the Second Realm who love the possessor, such as a past parent, sister, brother, husband, wife, child or friend. The possessor may respond to them more readily. At times the possessing soul might not even know that it has died. The mentor-exorcist should instruct the responding loved ones from the Second Realm to speak to the possessor. Then the mentor-exorcist must speak to the possessor, telling the possessor to go with the loved ones which it sees, having no fear in going with them.

If the room physically becomes disturbed with objects moving, lowering temperatures, or if the body of the victim begins shaking, the mentor-exorcist *must* reaffirm to the mentor-exorcist's own mind the ever-presence of Creative Love in *all* of creation. The Master demonstrated it when he calmed the waves of the tempestuous sea, declaring, "Greater works than I can you do" (John 14:12). It is then wise for the mentor-exorcist to say *aloud* with a firm and kind voice, 'Be still and know that *I Am*.' (Ps. 46:10) Be still in the presence of Creative Love. Be still and know that this is not your rightful place. Be still and know that a better place is prepared for you. Be still and know that you are loved. Be still and see those who are near you. Be still and go with them to the beautiful place which Creative Love has prepared especially for you wherein to find love and peace. Be still and go with them." Needless to say, it is easier to penetrate a fortress than the will of a stubborn conscience; however, remember that a fortress can be entered easily and properly by those in charge and, as Creative Love's faithful servant, you are in charge.

Hopefully possession is only temporary, but unfortunately, in extremely severe cases there may be no help except by the passing away of the victim or *even the mentor-exorcist if the mentor-exorcist is not sufficiently strong!!!* (Just as it is possible for a physician upon Earth-Eden to die from a patient's disease if the physician is too weak or not properly protected.) *Do not* be fooled; there is no devil. There are evil and sick souls who are earthbound and who, through their free will, can cause the effects of hell upon themselves and others just as righteous and healthy souls can, through their free will, cause the effects of heaven upon themselves and others.

Not every case of possession can be cured just as not every case of physical illness can be cured. Each of you is working off the Karma of self to become at-one with Creative Love through entering Grace. Follow daily in the steps of the Pathshower mentally, physically and spiritually and you will *not* walk astray.

In very unfortunate and very rare cases where possession cannot be exorcised, it does, however, come to an end when the victim dies just as cancer comes to an end when its victim dies. We realize in all compassion for you, our reader and student, that this is perhaps one of the saddest and most difficult aspects of human life to accept, and it is precisely with compassion in which you must understand it. Once there is no more flesh, there is no possession, nor cancer, for in the higher spiritual realms these sadnesses do not exist. Remember that even as Jesus suffered while upon Earth-Eden, then rose above materialistic concepts to the highest of Creative Consciousness, so is this possible for each of you. Pain does not last forever, grief does not last forever, and as you slowly give up self, you give up Karma and progress through kindness, compassion, honesty, justice, respect and equality and enter Grace through Creative Consciousness. You may not know what Karma a possessed victim was working off from past incarnations, perhaps even inviting the possessing soul and, in this difficult manner, was attempting to meet self. This is *not* the way, for it demonstrates neither kindness nor compassion.

Understand that all souls have free will and that you would not want it otherwise. The flesh is but temporal and the soul immortal; be progressively creative.

Chapter 18
Creative Progression

So much has been said, debated and written about creation that we plan to make this a very short chapter. Since this book is one to "set-the-record-straight" let us begin by saying that Creative Love is not sitting on almighty laurels, Creation is *not* completed, has not ended, will *never* end. Creation has never had a beginning and will never have an ending, since it reflects the handiwork of Infinite Intelligence which also has never had a beginning and never will have an ending. Creation constantly evolves. There is constant evolution of the spiritual and the physical and all that which is seen and unseen. There are endless situations, realms and planes of existence varying in forms and frequencies which are simply not possible to explain in this very limited vehicle known as words.

To give you an idea of some of the possibilities of existence, look at these words: solids, fluids, gases and plasmas. These are but four categories which try to explain the physical. There are many more categories which try to explain the spiritual. We have looked at only two realms, the physical and the spiritual; however, try to understand that there are realms which vary in status between spiritual and physical, which differ greatly beyond the physical and differ greatly beyond the spiritual.

Creation never ends because Infinite Intelligence is Ever-Creating! Creative Love never slumbers, never sleeps (Ps. 121:4); therefore, creation is constant. Its energies constantly evolve, are never lost, never end and never began; therefore, you are never lost, you never end, you never began. How then, you may ask, could you have been "created" if you never had a beginning?

"Creation" means much more than your dictionary gives it credit for. In reality it is not word-enough to fully explain the process.

We can best say Creation *"is"* as Creative Love *"is"* as you *"are."* For as Infinite Intelligence is the *"I Am"* (Exod. 3:14), all Creation is the *"it is;"* therefore, you also are the *"is"* or the *"are"* or the *"we"* or the *"us"* or the *"I Am."* Can you begin to understand the idea now, even with the limitation of words? You *"are;"* therefore, be thankful for Creative Love, the Loving *"I Am"* for *"being"* and for permitting you to *"be,"* thus we all are part of the *"I Am"* or *"what is!"* So be it! So it was! So it is! So it shall be! Creation without end! Amen!

We are not trying to confuse you but, again, words are not vehicles enough to explain Creation, or Creative Love. The ancients had the same difficulty and simply settled for *"I Am"* (Exod. 3:14) or "The One That Is, Is The One That Is," and so it is with Creation, for Creation is all that is, all that ever was and all that ever shall be, without end, ever evolving, ever progressing, and all of you, as all of us, are a part of Creation, which is everything.

Perhaps it might help somewhat in explaining to ask you to imagine the opposite, or "nothing!" Can you ever begin to imagine "nothing?" It is much easier to imagine, thus understand, "something." Now try to imagine, even though you may not understand, "everything!" In this manner, you can begin to understand creation and you can begin to progress in that understanding of what Creation is.

Let your mind wander, let your thoughts soar to mental heights unknown to you before; then by small yet constant soarings, you will begin to understand Infinite Intelligence more, you will begin to understand Creation more, you will begin to understand yourself more and you will also begin to create more.

First you will create better thoughts, then better usage of words and last, you will create better deeds, thus begin to use your creative abilities more progressively.

Infinite Intelligence has given you free will and has also given you your co-creative abilities. Use them fully and properly. Follow Creative Love's way of progressive evolution.

A human child which is created by its parents has a beginning and an ending, for it is namely a flesh-vessel; however, the soul which it houses has no beginning or ending. Here, once more, is an evolution or a changing of energy from one form to another for only a short period of time. At the time of the change called death, the creative energy of the soul does not die; rather, it changes form and continues to evolve, to progress, to become more enlightened and more reflective of Love's creations which do not have a beginning nor an ending.

The Old Testament states that Infinite Intelligence created the world in seven days. Remembering that a day in the courts of eternity is as a million eons and a million eons are as a day can help you to realize that this immeasurable amount of energy did not just pop into existence but that it always existed and constantly changes form in evolution, and as the scriptures state, "Even if heaven and earth pass away, My Word will last forever" (Matt. 24:35). Should this firmament and celestial pass away, Creation would not end, for its energy would continue in the unlimited energy of Infinite Intelligence, or Creative Love in another astonishing manner and you, as well as we, will still be a part of it, will still have our place in it, will still have the constant loving opportunities to become perfect as Infinite, Intelligent, Creative Love is perfect. Remember, "Eye has not seen, ear has not heard, nor has it entered into the thoughts of humans what Love has already prepared for those who progress in soul" (1 Cor. 2:9); therefore, soar for the empyreal in ethereal Creative Conscious through the priceless gift which you have, free will.

Chapter 19
Free Will Progression

Peace, freedom and free will have been the virtues upon which the more progressive civilizations have built their hopes and laws. A person who commits a serious offense to your society is often punished by means of imprisonment. Since all you souls were given free will by Creative Love, you have never wanted it taken away from you; yet it is you who build large cages of confinement called zoos for the wild beasts, and small cages for the birds, and aquariums for the fishes, and tethers of chains to hold so-called domestic animals, thus depriving them of their own birthright gift of free will and preventing them from working out their group-soul Karma!

But that's the way it is, you say! But suppose it is you who is denied your free will! You shoot wild game calling it "sport" and pull fish in nets to suffocate. You slaughter to eat the fowl and animals raised by human hands. But that's the way it is, you say! But suppose it is you who is eaten for food! True, that is the way it is, but that is *not* the way it should be. Don't you realize that this makes Earth-Eden hell? But it cannot change, you say! But it *can*, and *we know it can!!!* Why do some humans eat other humans? Why do some humans eat animals? Why do some humans eat vegetation? Why do some animals eat each other? Why do some animals eat vegetation? Why do some plants eat insects? Why? Why? Why? To live? That's life? For how long? Is there no better system? Of course there is!

Those who hunger and thirst for spiritual righteousness shall be filled by receiving spirituality and, after the change called death, they shall no longer need physical food but, unfortunately many still crave for food after they have died. (Only in the Second Realm.)

At this point some of you may be questioning us greatly, but let us ask you a few simple questions. Do you really believe that Infinite

Intelligence eats what it has created?? Do you really believe that it has someone slaughter physical life for it as food? Do you really believe that it eats or drinks?

As long as you are in the flesh, many will desire the flesh in various ways. It is with the realization that this should end after physical death that you can elevate your soul in progression now, overcoming much Karma, and advance quickly in Creative Consciousness. That is true free will! It may seem to some of you that in actuality we are asking you to give up your free will of desires, but what we are really asking you to do is to use your free will to the fullest of its potential through Creative Consciousness.

Food, for the severely overweight, can be an addiction just as well as alcohol, tobacco, drugs, sex, and gambling. But we are *not* suggesting that you stop eating and drinking. We are *not* suggesting that you become vegetarians overnight; although to become vegetarians very slowly would be a progression of great significance. The less flesh desired of the flesh, the more spiritual you will become. We *are* suggesting for you to take time to understand that one day after the change called death, you will not have to kill life in order to live. Prepare yourself along this line of thinking.

Can you imagine a world with kindness, compassion, honesty, justice, respect and equality without the destroying of animals, minerals, or vegetables? Without destroying *anything?* Think about it! Why is this not the way upon Earth-Eden? We hope you have progressed far enough through reading this book to realize the answer yourself!

Believe us when we tell you that this too shall pass away (this type of earthly existence). The physical is but a temporary shadow, an illusion in time. There is a greater life awaiting you beyond the grave. Have no fear of passing over in your due time, for you have done so many times before; but this time be more prepared so that you *need* not return. Strive to elevate spiritually to such an extent that you will not *wish* to return. Strive so that you will progress to realms unknown to your soul thus far; for eye has not seen, ear has not heard, nor can the heart imagine what Infinite, Intelligent, Creative Love has prepared for those who truly do demonstrate properly the free will given to them (1 Cor. 2:9). What is yours for the taking is *presently* beyond words!

In the present, eat what you need in order to sustain physical life (but do not make a glutton of yourself), and help feed the starving upon Earth-Eden. Your free will gives you that right and that ability. Remember that, "You *are* your brother's and sister's keeper" (Gen. 4:9). You may *have been* your brother or sister in a past incarnation, or you may be your sister or brother in the present or future incarnation. "Feed my lambs" (John 21:15), said Jesus. Will you do it? Whether you do, or whether you do not, will be known to Creative Love. What is your answer? Will you strive to be an angel?

Chapter 20
Angel Progression

There are angels among you who, through their Creative Conscious concern for you, have re-entered upon Earth-Eden not because they were again pulled into the force of the wheel of Karma, but rather because they are highly enlightened souls who have progressed through loving trust in Creative Love and have obtained Grace. They are "those among you" who wish prayerfully (as we do) to help guide you in the flesh to Creative Consciousness for your eventual return to Creative Love. We know you wonder who we are and why the use of the plural. For the present, let us remind you of what we have told you before: *Me* is *I*, and *I* is *I Am*, and *I Am* is *Us*, and *Us* is *We*. This is not meant to be a confusing answer. Meditate upon it now and we shall explain it in greater detail as we continue.

Try to understand your own place within the cosmos, try to understand other humans' places, try to understand a higher soul's place, try to understand the place of Jesus who was the highest demonstrator of Creative Consciousness. Since Infinite Intelligence is the only source and the channels are many (*all* can be channels), it must be understood that the higher a soul advances, the less value is given to names of past reincarnative entities of Earth-Eden as those souls unfold more to Creative Consciousness.

Many of those higher souls have never been in human bodies and are of the majority of souls which did not stray nor enter the flesh. They dwell in higher realms and at times assist those upon Earth-Eden and those in lower realms in various ways, such as writing books through channeling, or aiding souls in endless, progressive, spiritual tasks or missions on personal and national levels. Some also become "those among you" by taking on human bodies through the natural manner (incarnation) to live among you and to help bring Peaceful

Love into action for specific purposes. Then there are also those highly advanced souls who once were rebels but have stopped the reincarnative cycle through Creative Consciousness, have entered Grace and returned to the majority of souls which did not rebel. Some of these are those who may be called "Angels" or "Souls of Grace."

I interrupt these writings to share with you another transcript of a tape-recorded inspirational speaking session while in an enlightened state of consciousness:

"Infinite, Intelligent, Creative Love, I come to You seeking information as I attempt this session of speaking while in an enlightened state of consciousness. I pray for protection of my body and soul during this time. I ask that the information be for the wisdom of soul progression, and for guidance, in the name of Infinite, Intelligent, Creative Love. Amen.

"Clear the mind."

The mind is clear.

"Please go to where, to whom, as messengers of Creative Love, for the information which I ask for this session and tell me when you are ready."

We are ready.

"Please give information pertaining to the chapter of Angel Progression dealing with "those among us," and reveal from whom and from where this information comes. Thank you."

The soul of every entity upon Earth-Eden can leave its body when trained to do so or when the need arises, be it through a shock, an accident or through what seems to be a dream. Each soul can go to where it must for the information necessary for its progression, such as the soul of our channeling instrument Curt, and can travel to various places where some of the past skeins of time are revealed. Curt has gone to the Third and Fourth Realms for information included in these writings.

"Those among you," although perhaps a cliche, is a fact! There are those souls, some who were originally rebels, who through various reincarnations upon Earth-Eden have progressed to such a high degree that they choose to come back for special purposes and missions. There are also "those among you," known as angels, who have never rebelled and may never have been in human form, who can also come into the Earth-Eden plane for these missions.

"Human beings" is a synonym for rebellion and a calming factor is needed for this rebellion called human life. It is the attempt of angel guides to calm you humans, to calm your rebellion so that you will realize your oneness with Creative Love and return to Grace. If you could imagine Earth as Eden, then you would not need "those among you." They are there to help as doctors, statesmen, educators, missionaries, and as ordinary individuals whom many of you would least suspect. They all are guides among you whether they were in human form at one time or not. Realize that there *are* "those among you!"

There are also "those among you" who are not visible and who are not in human forms. At times this may be a person who has loved you while in the flesh and is coming back for a special purpose, to guide or comfort you. There are times when "those among you" may be very, very wise souls who have progressed beyond your present comprehension and are here for those in need of spiritual and physical guidance.

We have not given you any names and, therefore, you wonder who we are. How difficult it is to explain, for when one has risen far away from matter, away from Earth-Eden, away from greed, names are not necessary. But soon we will give you a name just for the sake of your understanding. However, as to the question of who we are—we are angels.

Picture us as at a very large oval table, seating anywhere from twelve to twenty individuals. We are souls who have progressed; some of us are souls who have been among you. We are channeling this information to our instrument, Curt. Where do we get it from? We are in the Third Realm where this information comes to us from various realms. Consider us a switchboard of advanced spiritual teachers consolidating our information like a computer; however, a computer of love, a computer of heart, a computer which knows its origin: our Loving God. God is Creative Love, God is Infinite Intelligence, the Source, the *only* Source!

We say to you with corrective love that "We are We." Names need not mean anything now. Some of us were formerly humans upon Earth-Eden, and some were formerly entities elsewhere; it doesn't matter. We are striving towards oneness with the Almighty and with all others. Rest assured, if we give you some of our past names, it would be a distraction, and only lead you to approve or disapprove of the lives which some of us have lived upon Earth-Eden. We have risen above that. We still have personalities, but they are personalities of our individual souls and not of any specific incarnation. We now are wiser, more complex and more advanced personalities with greater ability to love, forgive and teach. We are still progressing. As we are now, so someday you too may be. Prepare to follow us.

However, as promised, we shall give you the name of one of "those among you." The name is "Dorata;" it means "goldenly faithful." Soul names are the names by which the soul is referred to in the Akashic Records. They can be changed as the soul progresses for they are soulfully descriptive. Dorata is neither male nor female; rather, a soul not of human nature, (never having entered the flesh), and never having had the human nature of those who have been upon Earth-Eden. Dorata is what you would call an angel, a soul which has constantly progressed higher in Creative Consciousness to the state of Grace, one who has never entered Karma because of self (selfishness) or greed but has constantly progressed to perfection in the spirit and is at one with Creative Love.

Dorata is, as far as time goes, countless billions of years old. Now we realize that this is difficult for you to accept, but you can, if you but think back in meditation to the time before you rebelled. How old do you think your soul is?

Dorata is an angel of mercy. You've heard the phrase "angel of mercy," and now you will meet one. Dorata is without form and cannot be seen by human eyes. Perhaps this may be difficult to understand; therefore, let us explain:

Dorata does not play a harp, does not sit on a cloud. Dorata is total love, totally Creative Love's reflection. Try to understand the state of being neither male nor female, try to understand the absence of lust, the absence of sin, the absence of greed, the absence of selfishness, the absence of want. What is in its place in Dorata? It is the opposite of all those things; it is love, kindness, concern, goodness and giving.

Dorata spends all its time in homes and in institutions ministering faithfully to help those who have had severe reincarnations and are mentally and physically handicapped. The reason we mention Dorata is because Dorata has been working with an entity upon Earth-Eden whose name we do not wish to divulge for the sake of privacy and growth. The entity's present soul name is "Durack" which means "Here I am" and that is how we will refer to this entity. Dorata has been working with Durack for several incarnations. Durack is known to our channeling instrument, Curt, and has been quite a rebellious soul. Curt, whose present soul name is "Kielahn" which means "kindness," was also a rebellious soul, having entered the flesh eons ago, but a soul who has progressed highly in Love. It is possible that this could be the last reincarnation for Kielahn, and, if so, he will most likely stay very close to Earth-Eden for a long period of time after his passing, re-entering upon Earth-Eden only by choice to accomplish special missions, having overcome Karma, entering Grace and then too, may be one of "those among you."

Durack, Kielahn and others have known Dorata in several incarnations. Dorata, in golden faithfulness, constantly tries to penetrate the stubbornness of the soul of Durack. Durack has gained some spiritual progression in this incarnation, even though being severely handicapped. Durack in this incarnation has learned to smile, has learned to be appreciative, has learned to love, and to the blessed benefit of all, has learned to pray!! Understand what prayer is; it is that entity's acceptance and acknowledgement of Creative Love, its realizing that it did not create itself, something which the entity or the soul of Durack had never established since its rebellion eons ago before Atlantis. Durack still needs much spiritual growth although there has been much soul progression in this incarnation under the constant guiding force of Dorata.

Though Dorata has no form for the human eye to behold and neither can be heard, Dorata can be felt within the consciousness and the subconsciousness of Durack. You may think that a fortress is difficult to penetrate; however, it is seventy times seven thousand times more difficult to penetrate the heart of an unwilling soul! Why is it so difficult? Because *all* souls are created in the image of Creative Love and therefore have free will. A small percentage of rebels rejected Creative Love, and selfishly thought that they could do better as co-creators with no co-existence. Realize that "those among you" have tremendously difficult tasks, and they, like Infinite Intelligence, neither slumber nor sleep. However, at times they do need rest and do return to their various higher realms for regeneration, leaving well-qualified temporary replacements in their stead. Often when they take leave they depart in groups, creating the gathering of a great amount of spiritual energy. This energy can be visible to the eyes of certain privileged humans who are susceptible to its vibration. Often the "lights in the heavens" are the ectoplasms of "those among you."

Some of the UFO sightings are manifestations of this angelic or spiritual energy. There are UFOs of many differing characteristics. Some reported sightings are materialistic and some are spiritual energy. Some are even souls from the Atlantean era, who left Earth-Eden and are in various areas of the physical universe. Having developed to a point where they are not quite physical and not quite spiritual they are difficult to monitor or record correctly on your radar screens. For proof, go to the book of Ezekiel and you shall find it (Ezek. 1:4-28). You shall find not only the forms with the wheels, but also proof of many other things which are beyond our present subject. Some which Ezekiel mentioned were Atlanteans whom he did not mention by name, for you must remember that he knew not the word

"Atlantean," even though the Atlanteans existed many thousands of years before him. Ezekiel was in what can best be described as the "digging out from under" era. The rising and falling of civilizations has occurred many times upon Earth-Eden and can happen again according to human progression or regression!

We are finished at this time. You will awaken feeling fully refreshed in soul and in body with our prayers for blessings upon you, upon this work, and upon us. Awaken to full consciousness, Awaken.

I was indeed surprised with this session mentioning the soul of Durack whom I readily accept as an entity whom I love and care for. Once more it is shown that we all are related and that we most certainly are our own sisters' and brothers' keepers regarding their physical welfare and spiritual growth.

Trust and love (not blind faith in a temperamental deity), are basic factors in overcoming human greed and stubbornness. *Trust* in never-wavering Infinite Intelligence is the trust which is the opposite of fear (fear being nothing more nor less than the lack of trust in Infinite Intelligence). This trust abolishes your fear of the future and also abolishes your regrets of the past. The same is to be said about needless anxiety or worry, for anxiety and worry do not build soul progression; rather they eat away at the worrier. *Silent* meditation is the helper; by meditating upon Creative Love, you confess its existence and power. Continue in this progression and your trust will grow, for trust is progression as progression is trust.

Although millions of people attend their various houses of worship weekly, a constant lack of ethics with little spiritual growth continues in the world's politics, business practices, sexual morality and social justice. Governments try either to forbid religions, create state religions, or say that they believe in the separation of religion and state, then try to influence politics with religious ideas and religion with political ideas.

Whether on a personal or national level, good values and ethics are of great importance. Before good values and ethics can be practiced on a national level, they must first be practiced on a personal level.

All must come to the realization that there is only one purpose for human life upon Earth-Eden, and one way to achieve that purpose; through Infinite Intelligence! Your purpose is to progress enough in soul to return from where you strayed eons ago. The only way to achieve your purpose is to trust and practice Creative Love's teachings of kindness, compassion, honesty, justice, respect and equality.

Be not dismayed, for as only a little leaven will cause the entire dough to rise, so only a few of the enlightened *can* help to advance the spiritual epoch for humanity. Then, slowly but surely, by reversing the trend of satisfying self to the trend of helping others on a sure foundation of trust in Infinite Intelligence, will the eternal millennium of *creative, loving peace* be ushered in!

In what has been accepted as the ritual of communion in various churches, the words "body and blood" have been taught to have many meanings. Let us say that perhaps one of the soulfully progressive ways to consider these words is this:

Body as bread.
Bread as spiritual strength gained from trust in Creative Love.
Blood as wine.
Wine as spiritual wisdom gained from trust in Infinite Intelligence.

The Galilean Pathshower did *not* wish for a cannibalistic ritual to be established by having children taught to "eat his body and drink his blood!!" He wanted you to teach your children how to get along with each other, to love each other, to commune with each other, to *live* in communion with Creative Love, to live in harmony with all of the various religions, black, white, yellow, red, tan, rich, poor, young, old, male, female, heterosexual and homosexual. This is the beginning of communing spiritually in Creative Consciousness. As the Master said, "How can you say that you love your heavenly Father (Creative Love) whom you have not seen, if you do not love your brothers (and sisters) whom you *have* seen?" (1 Jn. 4:20). He also said, "Who are my brothers and sisters but those who do the Will of our Heavenly Father" (Matt. 13:48-50), and "Do this in remembrance of Me" (1 Cor. 11:25)! Therefore, realize that he wanted *all* to remember his teachings in thought, word and deed three times a day at each meal and to constantly progress in soul through Creative Consciousness as he did.

Open your eyes spiritually; look at the scriptures in the *spiritual* light. Millions are starving spiritually because of materialistic misinterpretations of the scriptures. "Feed my lambs" (John 21:15), he commanded his disciples, and we today are still trying! Seek the light of enlightenment from these spiritual teachings through Creative Consciousness. The righteous who hunger and thirst for spiritual food will be filled (Matt. 5:6). When reading the scriptures or other works of goodness written ages ago or in the present day, always ask yourself how they can enlighten you spiritually today to help you and others in soul progression.

Physical bodies will *not* rise up from the grave after they have decayed. The dust of the flesh returns unto the soil. The soul, however, continues. The dead *shall* come forth from their graves in resurrection *spiritually*, not physically. Those who were dead to Creative Consciousness shall come forth from mental ruts which are nothing more than graves with the ends knocked out. The Master said, "Let the dead bury the dead" (Matt. 8:22). He was *always* concerned about a person's soul and was speaking spiritually. The dead of which he spoke were dead, non-progressive ideas. Make every day your Christmas of rebirth under the enlightenment of the example of the Pathshower, the Star of Bethlehem. Make every day your Easter of bursting forth from the mental tomb of doubt into spiritual resurrection. Make every day your Ascension of soulfully rising heavenward in Creative Consciousness.

It is Love that promotes this enlightenment. Human love transforms; Creative Love transcends. Human love transforms a person to do good deeds and acts of mercy; Creative Love transcends human love to see above the material toward the spiritual for soul progression. Therefore, when you meditate, do not beg Creative Love to accept your liturgical sacrifice, for rather than any liturgical sacrifice, Creative Love wishes for you to demonstrate Creative Consciousness in your daily life! This progression can only be reached by giving up selfishness (self) through a trusting love in Infinite Intelligence.

There are "those among you" who constantly teach these lessons to you. We are not trying to make a mystery of "those among you," rather we are trying to impress upon you the value of their teachings. We love you and hope for you to "Love one another" (John 15:12,17) in order to eventually return home. Creative Love wishes for no one to perish (2 Pet. 3:9); therefore, strive for higher soul progression by treating *all* people equally. Strive for your progression to enter Grace.

Chapter 21
Grace Progression

The highest principle of Infinite Intelligence is the Law of Grace. Grace is two-fold. One, it is attained when a soul rejects the second-highest Law of Karma (cause and effect which continues reincarnation) by giving up self through Creative Consciousness. Two, it is a gift from Creative Love to all souls. This means that it is always there for each soul's taking, if the soul but gives up its selfish ways. It is often easier to live it than to perceive it, for Grace *is* the beginning of at-one-ment with Infinite, Intelligent, Creative Love which surpasses all human understanding (Phil 4:7).

Gravity is that force of attraction between all particles or bodies or that acceleration of one toward another. This is a simple explanation of gravity; however, it would take volumes to explain it fully and so it is with Grace. Strange as it may seem, this short explanation of gravity could also explain Grace. One could rephrase it to read: Grace is that force of compassionate attraction between all souls or bodies or that acceleration of one toward another in giving up self of which the return of the soul to Creative Love is an example, if that soul but progresses to do so!

Grace is explained by some religions as a supernatural gift from God which humans have no claim or right to. To that our reply is *"rubbish!"* We say to you that Grace is Creative Love. Grace is Unlimited, Just, Love. Grace is the final result of the highest form of Creative Consciousness which is not only your soulful birthright but yours to demand for yourself as an offspring of Creative Love. Grace is Nirvana. Grace is Heaven. Grace is not just the state of being without sin for a short earthly period of time, before sinning again; it is *no sin*! It is being perfect in soul as Creative Love is Perfect. It is the highest principle of Infinite Intelligence and the end of the reincarnative cycle.

It means one hundred percent of caring for others and for yourself. It means loving your enemies and doing good to those who spitefully use and abuse you (Matt 5:44). It means demonstrating soul progression. Grace is at-one-ment with Infinite, Intelligent, Creative Love achieved through the practicing of Creative Consciousness in thought, word and deed as demonstrated by the Master Pathshower.

Grace is *not* a supernatural gift that through Jesus' death gives you mystical points on an overstructured religion's score-card of existence. It is the result of your letting go of selfish ways as did the Pathshower, and entering the state of Grace. Grace *must* be earned. It is not to be confused with forgiveness. Forgiveness is freely given by Creative Love and by highly progressed souls in Creative Consciousness; but this does not mean that a wrong is forgotten without correcting it or without contrition. Only *then* can Grace be entered into, not before! This sanctifying Grace is absolutely necessary for *all* in order to end reincarnation. There is nothing supernatural about Grace, rather it is simply what Creative Love wants for you and is what you should want for yourself.

The opportunity for leaving the justice of Karma and entering the state of Grace is constant; the door of reformation is always open, even after the change called death. Since "*now* is the day of your salvation" (2 Cor. 6:2), now is the time for you to progress your soul higher and higher through Creative Consciousness. One of the main reasons for human life upon Earth-Eden is to progress in soul beyond Karma, into Grace, for at-one-ment with All Kind, Compassionate, Honest, Just, Respectful, Equal, Infinite, Intelligent, Creative Love.

We repeat: Grace is not forgiveness; it is the result of correcting your regressions after having asked for forgiveness, after having been forgiven, after regressing no more. It is the reaching of the highest enlightenment through Creative Consciousness which one attains when Karma has ended through equality.

Chapter 22
Equality Progression

All have been created with equal Love! This fact is *not* to be doubted, for Creative Love plays no favorites! (Could you imagine if that were the case?!) The inequality which exists upon Earth-Eden is human-made.

All of you have been created equal souls with free will, and each of you are in your present situation of life as the result of either your greed or your kindness. As you lose greed (the root regression) and gain kindness (the root progression), you can enlighten your soul more and more through Creative Consciousness, eventually rising above the second highest Law of Karma (cause and effect). You then obtain the strength needed to reincarnate no more, thus beginning your journey spirit-ward, or home-ward to at-one-ment with Infinite, Intelligent, Creative Love. This can be achieved only through kindness, compassion, honesty, justice respect and equality.

Where have you heard that before? We know that we have repeated this message many times, but it cannot be repeated enough, for it sets the record straight in that it is the *only message*!

One revered and repeated group of words in the Old Testament is, "Hear, (*Shema* in Hebrew) O Israel" (Deut. 6:4). That is how it is recorded in the scriptures; however, it means: "Hear, listen, for God's sake pay attention!" And that is the preface for all of the scriptures. Whenever an advanced soul (one of "those among you") mentioned in the scriptures came upon Earth-Eden, the first task of that soul was to attract the attention of those in the flesh; therefore, listen!

It is only through equality that the flesh can progress in the flesh, because Infinite, Intelligent, Creative Love is Equality! It is only through equality that the spirit can progress in the spirit, because Infinite, Intelligent, Creative Love is Equality! Realize this Wisdom!

Creative Wisdom does not tramp the streets like a prostitute as portrayed in the book of Wisdom 6:12-16, "Resplendent and unfading is Wisdom, and she is readily perceived by those who love her, and found by those who seek her. She hastens to make herself known in anticipation of men's desire; he who watches for her at dawn shall not be disappointed, for he shall find her sitting by his gate. For taking thought of her is the perfection of prudence, and he who for her sake keeps vigil shall quickly be free from care; because she makes her own rounds, seeking those worthy of her, and graciously appears to them in the highways and byways, and meets them with all solicitude," rather, here is a Creative Conscious, enlightened transcript of it:

"Resplendent and unfailing is the wisdom of equality, and it is readily perceived by those who love and found by those who seek it. The wisdom of equality hastens to make itself known in anticipation of each soul's need; those who watch for it at the dawn of their lives shall not be disappointed, for it can be found at the womb-gate of birth. For taking thought of the wisdom of equality is the perfection of prudence and those who for its sake keep vigil shall quickly be free from the cause of guilt; because it makes its course seeking those who understand its value and graciously appears to those on the pathways of life and meets those with assistance and opportunity in one of the highest forms of personal and collective soul progression."

Each soul-entity must strive for equality toward *all* people upon Earth-Eden. In each daily contact, bring about the Infinite, Intelligent, Wisdom-Will of equality by ridding yourself of prejudice when dealing with age, gender, sexual orientation, race and religion.

The following is a transcription of the last tape-recorded inspirational speaking session which I held for this book. Be aware of the seriousness of the message:

"Infinite, Intelligent, Creative Love, I come asking for assistance in this chapter dealing with equality progression which all humans should have for each other. I ask for protection of my body and soul during this session so that I may continue to be a channeling-instrument bringing enlightenment to a troubled

Earth-Eden in the Name of Love. Amen.

Clear the mind.

The mind is clear.

Please go to where, to whom, to what to receive information for the chapter of this book dealing with equality progression and tell me when you are ready.

We are ready.

Equality is justice, equality is kindness, equality is free will, equality is all that which Infinite Intelligence is. Equality is the fairness with which all souls are to deal with each other and themselves, as is the manner in which Creative Love always has and always will deal with each of you.

Equality requires the absence of fear, which you already know is nothing more or less than the lack of trust in Infinite Intelligence. Once this has been achieved, and there is no lack of trust in Infinite Intelligence, then there is no lack of trust in your own possibilities.

Equality is demonstrated through free will. It is that which gives you the ability to function as Creative Love wishes you to function. Equality is the setting aside of self, the setting aside of ego, the setting aside of human will to do the proper Will of Creative Love through Creative Consciousness. As we have told you in the Preface, the word "Creative" means having the ability to bring into being that which evolves from a person's thinking as the Pathshower so greatly demonstrated, thus becoming the Path for all humans to follow. "Consciousness" means that part of you which is constantly aware (through the brain) of what the mind (which is the will of the soul) relates to. When put together as "Creative Consciousness", you can begin to realize the possible ideal or idea of Infinite Intelligence. This is the understanding of the Truth, the Love, the Infinite, the Intelligence within each one of you.

We shall continue in other areas of equality, but at this point before we do so, we find it quite important to have a proper and perhaps even a lengthy prologue in the beginning of this chapter. This is to emphasize that equality is what Infinite Intelligence is all about, what life is all about.

There are "those among you," who have obtained Creative Consciousness to a high degree and are trying most earnestly to bring this awareness to all souls upon Eden-Earth today. Those Angels must be listened to, must be heard, must be obeyed. Earth-Eden is presently in a dynamic yet crucial epoch of its history.

There is much, much need for spiritual and physical growth upon Earth-Eden at this time. The dangers of the physical are (as you all know) not so much the natural catastrophes which could occur, but the catastrophes which could be caused by human hands. War is *not* a *natural* catasphrophe! Spiritual concern can prevent this danger from becoming a reality. There is deep, deep need for spiritual growth upon Earth-Eden today. Many of your overstructured religions and political groups are not doing a proper job. Some religions and political groups are more interested in their names and methods than in their results and consequences. Look at your planet today; there are starving people, and these are starving at the hand of humans; this is *not* Infinite Intelligence!! This is *not* equality!!

Equality must begin with each of you. Equality must be in the foremost thoughts of every leader upon Earth-Eden today. Political and religious blindness *must* be set aside; bigotry *must* be set aside; if not, although Earth-Eden will not physically end, tremendous hardships and severe physical difficulties, such as famines, wars, destruction, and who knows what (and God shudders at what) will occur. Put your house in order; begin with your own soul and have trust in Creative Love. Remember that equality is a must for each and every soul to achieve for individual progression and each nation to achieve for collective progression.

Creative Love wishes that no soul should perish. Some souls upon Earth-Eden have reached exceedingly low levels of regression which have brought hardship, torture and death to millions of humans throughout history! This is nothing compared to what can happen! We do not wish for the book of Revelation to be fulfilled; it is *not* yet set in motion! *You can change it through Equality!! For your own sake, listen to us. What must we do to make you understand that your hardships, your evil, your greed, come from your own misuse of free will and not from Infinite, Intelligent, Creative Love!*

We are finished. With refreshment, with Love, with energy, with integrity, awaken to continue this work. Awaken."

After this session, a feeling of warning, yet hope, for all souls upon Earth-Eden stayed with me for a long period of time. I can not fully express my feelings, but I know that we are in the latter days upon Earth-Eden as we know it. What the outcome of the change will be is entirely up to us. Will it be disastrous or soul progressive? Let me now continue with the inspirational writing.

Infinite, Intelligent, Creative Love is ever concerned about you; there is nothing for you to fear except inequality. For inequality is unkind, uncompassionate, dishonest, condemning, unforgiving, disrespectful and soul-regressive into mental darkness, being quite the opposite of equality which is kind, compassionate, honest, forgiving, respectful, just and soul progressive in the mental light of Creative Consciousness, reflecting the perfect Will of Creative Love.

Age equality is usually not even given a second thought. Too many young people do not think that one day they too may be old, and too many old people forget what it was like to be young. Realize that a person (the entity in the flesh) has a limited physical life span. The soul, however, is ageless, for each physical baby houses a soul which is not new, and each old person who dies at the age of ninety is not a ninety-year-old soul, rather only a ninety-year-old person representing about one day in the life of an eternal soul. The soul does not end with the change called death, only the body does; therefore, realize that the only purpose of life upon Earth-Eden is for the soul's progression. Respect each other regardless of your ages, for each of you may have been or possibly will be of various ages in other reincarnations. It is only through the respect of equality that there can be great soul progression. You must deal fairly with each other.

Gender equality has slowly through the years begun to make headway. Gender bigotry has been enormous. Women have had to struggle from the dawn of history to break the unjust, ungodly ideas of male supremacy. Do you still not realize that Creative Love did *not* create you male or female? Creative Love created you as souls of spirit and not of flesh, rather in the image of Creative Love. The flesh is corruptible; Creative Love is not flesh, is not gender, it is Father-Mother, Parent Comforter. We use these words *only* for lack of better ones. Creative Love *loves, is*, and *loves you*! *You are! You are souls!* You are not just sexual objects! Render unto Creative Love what is Creative Love's for there is nothing else. Unfortunately, among the greatest offenders of gender equality are many of the overstructured religions in their false teachings of male supremacy; however, the enlightenment of the dawn of Creative Consciousness slowly but surely has begun in this your day. Respect each other regardless of your gender, for each of you may have been or possibly will be of the opposite gender in future reincarnations. It is only through respect of equality that there can be great soul progression. You must deal fairly with each other.

Sexual orientation is an equality which has suffered bigotry as no other form of equality and has also been wrongly condemned by the false teachings of many of the overstructured religions. Caring is the first step in doing. Homosexuals, learn to love heterosexuals. Heterosexuals, learn to love homosexuals. Be you heterosexual, homosexual, bisexual, asexual or celibate, learn to love each other, for when the flesh ends and the change called death occurs, there is no taking or giving in marriage (Mark 12:25), no sexual encounters as you know them to be upon Earth-Eden; rather, there is opportunity for the love of being at one with all of Love's creations, which is the primary purpose of progression. Learn to look beyond sexual orientation. Learn to look into each other's hearts as Creative Love does.

Whatever your sexual orientation, it does not make you virtuous, righteous, wrong or evil. Only your personal motives and behavior as a sexual individual can do that. Only if you are selfish and let your greed control your lusts to the point of hurting others does your sexuality become offensive. All relationships can have sexual progression when there is kindness, compassion, honesty, justice, respect and equality, thus elevating sexuality from an extension of self to the beautiful, loyal, tender concern for another soul.

Remember, no souls reincarnate against their will. Each soul which re-enters upon Earth-Eden in a new vessel of flesh does so because it wants to or has accepted to do so for further soul progression. Each of you is upon Earth-Eden in this present incarnation in order to work out past Karmas and has accepted your lot before you re-entered. Hopefully because of the various sexual situations in which you find yourselves, you will have learned your individual lessons and will enter into Grace and return to Creative Love, thus having to go out no more (Rev. 3:12). Acceptance plays a major role in these specific situations which allows equality progression. Respect each other regardless of your sexual orientation, for each of you either may have been or possibly will be of various sexual orientations in other reincarnations. It is only through respect of equality that there can be great soul progression. You must deal fairly with each other.

Race equality can only come about when no one race any longer foolishly, selfishly believes it is a chosen race, a superior race, a better race. Race equality can come about when a person of one skin color sees only the beauty of the variety of Love's colors rather than regressively thinking that one color is better than another. Imagine if Infinite Intelligence never created the various colors or the numerous shades; what a dull world it would be. Imagine if you were all of one race; imagine if you all had the same color eyes; imagine if you all had the same color hair! Do you think that you would get along any better with each other? Do you think that lack of variety of color would prevent greed? Do you want to limit the color of the races more through greed? You have already ended the Blue race!! "Those among you" come in various colors. Didn't you know that? Children love colors! Think as an innocent child; the Pathshower did! That is where you can begin to create more race equality. Respect each other, regardless of your various races, for each of you may have been or possibly will be of various races in other reincarnations. It is only through respect of equality that there can be great soul progression. You must deal fairly with each other.

Religious equality is certainly a paradox, for shouldn't religion and equality be the same? Unfortunately, where religion should be the root of equality, it is all too often, because of its overstructured organization, the weed of greedy iniquity! What value does a religion have when it foolishly believes that it has all the answers and, therefore, that all the other religions are wrong? What value does a religion have when it does not take care of orphans and the aged? What value does a religion have when it is prejudiced against the majority of the people upon Earth-Eden, namely women? What value does a religion have when it is bigoted to the various natural sexual orientations? What value does a religion have when it ignorantly claims one race to be above all others?

Overstructured religion, just as overstructured politics, falls far too short in its deeds of soul progression, which is supposed to be its *only* purpose. Creative Love does not wish for any sacrifices or litanies (Ps. 40:6,8). Creative Love does not wish for you to bend your knee in homage, rather *wishes* only for each soul to bend it's selfish will thereby progressing in soul through thought, word and deed in kindness, compassion, honesty, justice, respect and equality, thus leaving Karma, needing to reincarnate no more and entering Grace to become *at one* with Creative Love! Going home!

Let us give warning to the leaders of the various religions: *Creative Love is, watches, knows, loves, but also "Will not be mocked"* (Gal. 6:7)!!! Many pompous religious or political leaders have reincarnated into situations far from their greedy desires. Be warned! "*Now* is the day of your salvation" (2 Cor. 6:2)! Change, repent, open your hearts to equality *now*! Respect each other regardless of your religion, for each of you may have been or possibly will be of various religions in other reincarnations. It is only through respect of equality that there can be great soul progression. You must deal fairly with each other.

Never place the physical before the spiritual. Look into your hearts and minds to have progression through the ontological.

Chapter 23
Ontological Progression

God—Infinite, Intelligent, Creative Love—is the source of knowledge; therefore, the source of *your* knowledge. In knowing that Earth-Eden is not your goal nor your permanent home, progress to your utmost in *this* incarnation. Use the many opportunities for progression which greet you daily in *this* life; the growth and experiences which you encounter can be blessings unmeasurable. All that is forthcoming can be transformed into positive possibilities which will enrich your soul now and hereafter.

Learn to cultivate a calm and quiet temperament. Let peace of mind be your standard way of operation. Realize that you must give love in order to receive love, you must give happiness in order to receive happiness, you must forgive in order to be forgiven; you must be honest with others, for if you are not, then you are also not honest with yourself.

Truth is changeless; however, souls do change. Both are composed of endless, flowing energy. Souls have an individualness, yet a co-minglingness with all parts of the cosmic. The individual soul is not limited by the physical body, but can extend beyond time and space and co-mingle with all of creation, and can bring the goodness of Creative Love throughout the cosmic constantly and forever.

It need not be that the stars affect the entities, rather that the entities affect the stars. The stars are not to control you upon Earth-Eden; realize through your demonstration of the knowledge that Infinite Intelligence is Creative Love, that you are co-creators with free will, which when used progressively *can* move mountains (Matt. 17:20), ever creating, ever expanding the cosmos.

The prime function of that vehicle which temporarily houses the soul, known as the body, is to help enlighten the soul through learning from experiences. Experiences with others create a chain-reaction of shared experiences which result in learning opportunities for many souls.

You can mentally create learning opportunities by projecting or expanding your thoughts beyond a given situation, thus creating progressive learning possibilities depending upon development of your objectivity which makes use of the principles of the physical sciences and those of metaphysics.

With the inner drive of Creative Consciousness, one can create many staircases for mental and physical systems of elevation and induce the influence of Infinite Intelligence, thus resulting in a strength-gathering, restful inner peace which surpasses all human understanding (Phil. 4:7).

Peacefully extend yourself beyond your physical body and out into the cosmos with Creative Consciousness, then realize your endless possibilities as an equal member of the universe. This is not an anthropocentric world, rather a theocracy of the entire physical and spiritual cosmos. There are high progressions of life attained through free will with varying degrees of mental intelligence and spiritual unfoldment, all of which give constant opportunity now, and after the change called death, to continue to elevate, to progress beyond Karma, enter Grace through the limitless Creative Consciousness demonstrated by many and to the highest degree by the redeeming entity, your Pathshower.

Calm your lusts, calm your fears, and remember that Infinite Love is *always* with you even to the end of your world (realm) (Matt. 28:20) and always stays with you even through the following worlds (realms) through which you will progress until you reach *home.* Creative Love loves you so much that it was this Love which created you as an everlasting soul with free will to become perfect and at-one with Infinite Intelligence.

Remember that trust turns into obedience, obedience turns into altruism, and altruism turns into equality, therefore, keep turning, turning, turning until you have turned out right. As long as you have limited beliefs, you will have limited results. Make righteousness your goal, and cherish Infinite Truth and Kindness, while constantly checking your progression, and never be afraid to question.

Chapter 24
Question Progression

Why do some people die young as children rather than living a long life? Isn't this cruel?

Let us compassionately answer "yes" to the second portion of this question. A child's death is indeed a cruel and needless act! Cruel for all the obvious reasons, and needless because that is exactly what such a death is, needless.

Creative Love does not cut the entity's life short; the soul of that entity does!! How? Let us remind you that you have free will. That *each* of you *chose* to enter upon Earth-Eden; *none* were forced! Because you have not yet entered Grace and still exist under Karma, you *will* reap what you have sown in the present and previous lives (Gal. 6:7).

Let us explain: Before any soul enters upon Earth-Eden, it sets a goal for that incarnation. Whatever the goal may be, it is what that soul hopes to achieve in that particular lifetime. Suppose a soul greatly needs to learn humility, and re-enters upon Earth-Eden with that goal in mind, expecting it will take a life span of seventy years to achieve. However, the entity does not progress in learning humility, but begins to grow greedy for financial wealth and lives so until the age of sixty-five when all finances. Not being able to face living without the style to which the entity has foolishly grown accustomed, the entity commits suicide. We do not wish to comment any further about suicide other than in cases of young or healthy bodies, it is *one* of the *worst* regressions that a soul could commit. This leaves that soul in a serious situation. First, it has not achieved its goal; and second, it still has five years of earthly time allotted to achieve that goal.

Upon leaving its body in such a wrong way, the soul is counselled and attended to by various angels, learns that it must complete its earlier agreement, and re-enters upon Earth-Eden for another five years to continue striving towards humility. It has an excellent opportunity in its reincarnation to learn that as a child, and upon reaching its fifth year the soul passes out of that body. Realize that the little child which dies is an ageless soul that had left a five year old flesh vessel; and those who were closely associated with the sixty-five year old person as well as with the five year old child were all working out a specific individual and collectively intertwined Karma. The cruelness of suicide was afflicted on others by self (selfishness, root sin), and to self by self, not by Infinite Intelligence.

Will we meet our loved ones after the change called death?

Yes, in most cases, depending upon the soul progression of each of your individual loved ones, and depending upon your own soul progression. For those who have progressed in Creative Consciousness, there will be much joy, happiness and laughter in reunion with relatives, friends and loved ones in the Second Realm soon after having passed over. Those in the Second Realm will, in most cases, have foreknowledge of the advent of a new arrival, and often there is a wonderful reunion; however, some may have either re-entered upon Earth-Eden or progressed on to the Third Realm.

There are constant deaths from one realm and constant births into other realms. When you pass over you may never meet some relatives or friends of your family who died before you were born because they may have reincarnated upon Earth-Eden, or they may have been *you* in a past incarnation. This, however, will all be revealed to you after you have met self (been evaluated or judged) in the Second Realm when *all* of your previous incarnations are brought to full remembrance. Then *you* will make a decision how and where to continue your progression, be it to stay for a short or long period in the Second Realm, to progress on to the Third Realm, or to reincarnate again upon Earth-Eden. *You* will make these decisions after being aided by various angels, past loved ones and your own soul's mind!

What is the Holy Spirit?

The Holy Spirit is beyond human persona. It is the perfected essence of Creative Love. It is that spirit of holiness (Creative Consciousness), that spirit of kindness, compassion, honesty, justice, and equality which are the characteristics of Infinite Intelligence. It is doing the *Will* of Infinite, Intelligent, Creative Love. It filled the soul of the Master when he returned from Jordan (Matt 4:1), and went to spend many days in the solitude of the desert to commune with Creative Love, thus becoming more and more the Creative Demonstrator of Love's Perfection.

That same spirit of holiness, Creative Consciousness or Creative Love, stayed behind upon Earth-Eden in the acts of the apostles and the disciples after the Master returned to higher realms. This spirit is ever-present even today in each enlightened soul who has progressed to the point of constantly trying to overcome self. Humans can not really *live* (progress) without doing Creative Love's Will. The Master reminded himself of that Truth when he felt tempted. "It is written that one shall not live (progress) by bread (matter) alone but by every word of God (learning of the Holy, Spiritual Ways of Creative Love, then Living in that manner)" (Matt. 4:4).

Have all fallen through Adam (and Eve)?

Yes and no! Many souls who have entered the flesh upon Earth-Eden have fallen far away from Creative Love and its ways; however, the Pathshower proved that humans *can* live lives according to Creative Love, and thus can become purer in spirit. Remember *this* very important *truth: Each soul in the flesh has not been created in Adam or Eve's fallen image, rather in the image of Infinite, Intelligent, Creative Love which is unfallen* (Gen. 1:26)!

An unending source, Infinite, Intelligent, Creative Love constantly gives strength and opportunity to every living soul in the flesh with which to progress and elevate. When events in daily life seem not to be going properly, *remember your source*, remember that you can forever unfold in the reflection of the *true* image in which you are created; an *unfallen* image with an endless source of concerned *love.* The strength of your Creative Source is the resiliency with which you can set yourself upright to progress in spiritual and physical ways, *unfallen!*

What is the church?

What it is and what it should be are two very different things. In spiritual and physical actuality it should be living souls in the flesh upon Earth-Eden demonstrating Creative Consciousness; kindness, compassion, honesty, justice, respect and equality to *all* in thought, word and deed as established by the Pathshower Jesus, thus overcoming self, selfishness (the root sin) and entering Grace, returning to at-one-ment with Infinite, Intelligent, Creative Love.

Prayerful meditation, which the Master taught to be a vital part of life upon Earth-Eden, is the communing in thought with Creative Love. It is *not* a set form of words dully repeated, but a personal silent conversation in thought from the individual soul to Creative Love.

Silent meditation, which should always follow silent prayer, enables you to receive answers in thought from Creative Love through that "still small voice" (1 Kings 19:12,15). Once you have become accustomed to *listening* to Creative Love you will learn that the still small voice never lies to you. You may not always care for the answers, but through obedience you can learn that they bring assured personal soul progression.

What Jesus taught through Creative Consciousness is that Infinite, Intelligent, Creative Love never leads any soul into temptation. *It is not the tempter!!* What Jesus did teach was to *ask for protection*, to not lead oneself into temptation through materialistic, non-spiritual desires of *selfishness.* The prayer should read: "Protect us from being lead into selfish temptation."

Are there souls on other planets and in other galaxies?

1 Yes, but most are not in what you would consider human form. Some of them are mentioned in the book of Ezekiel in the Old Testament of the Bible.

Chapter 25
Bible Progression

In this chapter we explain various verses of the Old and New Testaments, but first we wish to remind you of the meaning of the word "testament." Perhaps the simplest way would be to replace it with the word "will;" the old and new will! When an entity upon Earth-Eden prepares for departure to the Second Realm, often a legal document is drawn up called the "will" or the "last will and testament," which testifies officially as to intentions of how and what should become of physical possessions which *cannot* be taken along with the entity upon the change called death. So it is with the library of books which are contained in the Bible. They are divided into three branches: the Old Testament which many foolishly think of as the old intentions of God, the New Testament which many foolishly think of as the new intentions of God, and the Apocrypha which many foolishly think is or is not God's intent to be considered holy scripture.

Much has been changed in the thousands of years which have passed since the numerous books were written. Several major over-structured religions have accepted many books to be their "Holy Writ," however let us remind you of what we said in Chapter 8, Justice Progression: "Not all religious books of the various religions are totally the Word of Infinite Intelligence, but like many books through the ages (as this one) are a mingling of the thoughts of Creative Love with those of souls (of various levels of progression) made manifest in words. They can be holy words only when they create a holy situation or result in kindness, compassion, honesty, justice, respect and equality, thus creating progression between humans and Creative Love, between humans and each other, between humans and all other creatures, plants and nature for which Infinite Intelligence intends progression in harmony."

We emphatically urge you always to seek the *spiritual* message of soul progression within these writings. *Always* seek Creative Consciousness and always apply it in your daily thoughts, words and deeds. Do this as you deal with yourself and others in your daily life within your present incarnation as an entity upon Earth-Eden who wishes for its soul to elevate, unfold and progress above the Law of Karma (cause and effect), then to enter Grace (at-one-ment with Love's Ways) in order to return to Creative Love, having to go out (reincarnate) no more (Rev. 3:12). This must become your goal!

To help set the record straight, we give you the following metaphysical interpretations of various scripture verses with Creative Conscious enlightenment.

"I can do all things in him which strengthens me." (Phil. 4:13)

These were the words which Paul wrote to the early Christians at Philippi. When one's mind is attuned to Creative Consciousness, one needs no blind faith, for then one *knows* and *understands* Love's Will and lives within its Laws; having overcome fear, which you well *know* by now as being nothing more or less than lack of trust in Infinite Intelligence. Creative Consciousness parts the waves of fear, creating the mental dryshod path of confidence for all whose minds are elevated to such enlightenment, as did Moses when he parted the Red Sea through Creative Consciousness. In Creative Consciousness you *can* do all progressive things of soul progression.

"Let your light so shine before men (all), so that they may see your good works, and glorify the Father (Creative Love) which is in Heaven." (Matt. 5:16)

These are the words which Matthew records as Jesus'; therefore, let your Creative Conscious thoughts, words and deeds excel in your life so as to shine forth like glowing examples to all with whom you come in contact, so that they may see in you the reflection of Infinite, Intelligent, Creative Love. Do not hide your good, candle-light deeds as regressions under a bushel basket, rather place them upon the candle-sticks of golden purity to enlighten all those in your home and in your life. This will prevent much stumbling for yourself and others in the darkness of being ignorant of Infinite Intelligence.

"What profited a person if they gain the entire world, but lose their soul?" (Matt. 16:26)

What could one possibly gain in exchange for one's soul? *Nothing!* There is absolutely *no* gain of any sort, rather it is a regression of the most extremely dangerous and lowest form. A lost soul is the result of the root regression, "self," meaning selfishness, greed, lust. The shadow of the severe doom of this action cannot be cast, however, without the light of Infinite, Intelligent, Creative Love which wishes for no soul to perish and *always* keeps the door of reformation open, both now and even after the change called death. Unfortunately, due to the stubbornness of some souls, this can take eons of time. Why? Because each soul has been blessed with free will and can either learn under Karma by cause and effect or enter Grace and progress free-willingly in Creative Love.

"Behold, I make all things new." (Rev. 21:5)

John writes these words of Revelation as being those of Infinite Intelligence. This is an excellent scripture lesson to keep in mind at the beginning of each new year, at the taking of a new position, or at the point of a change in one's life. A new time, a new challenge, a new concept equals a new *you*! Rebirth!

Infinite Intelligence constantly makes all things new. New opportunities constantly surround you because of the benevolent gift of free will which Infinite, Intelligent, Creative Love Lovingly gives to you. All can constantly be made new in that all can constantly expand, evolve and progress. Creative Love has not finished Creation, rather it is a continuing opportunity for growth in making all things new including you and the cosmos of which you are an equal part. There are no limits to the greatness of Infinite Intelligence, and there are no limits to your making yourself new to become perfect in soul as Creative Love is perfect.

"Our Father which art in Heaven,"

Infinite, Intelligent, Creative Love is *always* with us.

"Hallowed be Thy name."

As namesakes we have the free will to prove Holiness by our doing likewise.

"Thy Kingdom come."

Infinite Intelligence shows us the way to return home; it is up to us to follow.

"Thy Will be done on earth, as it is in Heaven."

By small yet constant steps through kindness, compassion, honesty, justice, respect and equality we can make Earth-Eden into paradise.

"Give us this day our daily bread,"

We *are* our sisters' and brothers' keepers; therefore, it is our duty to share our goods and talents with friend and stranger, thus feeding Creative Love's lambs both physically and spiritually.

"And forgive us our trespasses, as we forgive those who trespass against us,"

If we do not forgive, how can we expect forgiveness?

"And lead us not into temptation, but deliver us from evil,"

Protect us from being led into the error of selfish temptation. Only as we tempt others are we tempted in return by cause and effect, until we are tried by Creative Love and progress through Infinite Intelligence, thus entering Grace.

"For Thine is the kingdom, and the power, and the glory, forever and ever,"

Infinite Intelligence is constant Creative Consciousness pouring forth endless opportunities of limitless compassionate Love for *all* to become perfect in soul as Creative Love is perfect, *all* in *all.*

"Amen."

So it was, so it is, so it shall be forever and ever without beginning, without ending. (Matt. 6:9-13)

"God (Infinite Intelligent, Creative Love) is a Spirit (spirit of Perfect Holiness); and they (progressive, seeking souls) that worship (obey) Him (Infinite, Intelligent, Creative Love's laws) must worship (demonstrate) Him in spirit (thought, word and deed) and in truth (complete trust)." (John 4:24)

Spirit is not the physical as truth is not the lie. Worship is not the ritual one attends in a house of worship one day per week. Worship is living Creative Consciousness daily in the spirit of your thoughts, words and deeds. The actions of kindness, compassion, honesty, justice, respect and equality are the truth of worship, and ritualistic practice one hour per week in a house of worship without the daily practice of demonstrating Love's Will toward friend and stranger is the lie.

"God is Love." (1 John 4:8)

Creative Love *is*. Creative Love is Life. Life is Creative Love. Love is life as life is love. Without love there is no life, merely existence; for life is to progress. Without life there is no love, for love is to progress. Creative Love *is*. Creative Love is love. Creative Love is life. You *are*.

"Father, into Your hands I commend my spirit." (Luke 23:46)

These last few words which Luke says were spoken by Jesus during his tortuous physical pain can become for you a spiritually progressive affirmation when translated metaphysically in this manner: "Infinite, Intelligent, Creative Love, into Your Consciousness I commend my soul this day." Begin your day by speaking this statement out loud. Continue keeping Creative Conscious ideal-ideas in the forefront of your mind. Great soul progression *will* be gained by demonstrating the Master's teachings in doing the works of Creative Love in your daily actions with others, no matter how difficult some wayward souls may try to make it for you. Give their lack of trust in Infinite Intelligence and in themselves no strength through *your* doubt! Rather, remember that you are surrounded by Creative, Progressive Love, which comes from the only source which is Infinite

Intelligence and *Infinite Intelligence has no competition*!

It is by small yet constant steps that one helps wayward souls ascend the staircase of enlightenment; and that enlightenment *will* slowly but surely give those souls the needed encouragement with which toovercome *all* their needless fears. Therefore, begin and close each day by wisely, courageously, lovingly commending your precious soul into the Consciousness of Infinite, Intelligent, Creative Love.

"For He shall give His angels charge over thee, to keep thee in all thy ways." (Ps. 91:11)

Creative Love *has* given you angel-protection and guidance to help you progress in all your ways according to Infinite Intelligence. These ancient words of David came to the mind of the Pathshower as he was tempted by "self" in the wilderness. He also rebuked his own temptation by this Creative Conscious affirmation: "Thou shalt not tempt the Lord thy God" (Luke 4:12) "Tempt" can also be translated as "to be tried." Do not tempt (try) Creative Love, a love much greater than yours; rather try yourself in the furnace of that All-Mighty Love, to have the dross of "self" cast off in order to progress in Infinite Intelligence, "having to go out no more (reincarnate)," thus entering Grace.

"Therefore Eli said unto Samuel, 'Go, lie down, and it shall be if He (Infinite Intelligence) call thee, that thou shalt say, Speak, Lord; for thy servant heareth.' So Samuel went and lay down in his place (in the temple). And the Lord came, and stood, and called as at other times, 'Samuel, Samuel.' Then Samuel answered, 'Speak; Lord, for Thy servant heareth.'" (1 Sam. 3:9-10)

Eli of the Old Testament certainly gave Samuel soulful advice when the two of them were sleeping in the temple near where the ark containing the Commandments of their day were housed. The young Samuel thought Eli had called him several times in the night, and each time Eli said, "I did not call you Samuel." However, it was after the third time when Eli realized that the presence of Infinite Intelligence was being revealed to Samuel, and this realization gave Eli that ever-soul-progressive advice to tell Samuel to respond to that voice.

For those who seek Infinite Intelligence, often that still small voice of the Spirit of Love within your own temple becomes quite *audible*, and always remains quite persistent. It is especially so for those who live close to the teachings of Creative Love. However, it is not enough to hear the voice, and it is not enough to reply to the voice. You must *obey* those teachings of the voice to help yourself and others to progress in Creative Conscious demonstration of kindness, compassion, honesty, justice, respect and equality.

"This is the day which the Lord (Infinite, Intelligent, Creative Love) has made; let us rejoice and be glad in it." (Ps. 118:24)

Every day is the dawning of new opportunities from Creative Love for soul progression; therefore rejoice, be glad, be cheerful in this truth. Show enthusiasm with which to elevate your spirit to Creative Consciousness as you help others to do the same. Demonstrate your birthright of reflecting Creative Love in your daily co-creative powers through kindness, compassion, honesty, justice and equality.

Every day can be your Christmas, your rebirth. Every day can be your Ascension, your rising above your past. Today is great with all the wonderful things which Creative Love has prepared, and it is waiting for you simply for the taking. Strength, happiness, comfort, health, friendship and prosperity are all yours if you but show enthusiasm and an open heart through your thoughts, words and deeds, to the Will of Infinite, Intelligent, Creative Love. This is the day! This is the day for great soul progression to enter Grace and for you to begin your journey homeward, to be at heavenly oneness with yourself, others and Infinite Love.

"Be not conformed to this world but be transformed by the renewing of your mind (through Creative Consciousness) that you may prove what is that good and acceptable and perfect Will of God (Infinite Intelligence, the likeness into which you also may progress)." (Rom. 12:2)

Paul wrote these words in his letter to the early followers of the

Master in Rome. Too bad they did not heed that wise advice, rather than, in centuries to come, dragging the conformation of the physical world into the so-called overstructured religion which *they* established, instead of trying to follow Creative Love. Realize that you are *in* this world (realm) but not *of* this world (realm). You are all souls of spiritual Love, therefore as spiritual beings, begin to conform to Infinite Intelligence. Spiritual progression is soul progression. Leave materialistic trinkets by the wayside on your path through this incarnation, for you can take *nothing* physical with you through the change called death.

"Let this mind (Creative Consciousness) be in you, which was also in Christ Jesus (Jesus demonstrating Creative Consciousness)." (Phil 2:5)

Paul wrote these words in a letter to the early followers of the Master at Philippi. Creative Consciousness is the highest standard of thought for any human in that it asks itself the question in each situation, "What does Infinite Intelligence want me to do?" Keeping this in mind, Creative Consciousness becomes more a part of you (your soul) as it also became fully part of the Pathshower. It is for the progression of your soul to *want* to think, speak and act in the manner of Creative Love. Let this mind of Creative Consciousness which was demonstrated by the Master become your mind, your way of thinking, speaking and acting. The benefits achieved by this consciousness will enrich your present life many times over. A bright and enlightened future is yours, simply for the thinking, for the saying, for the doing.

"In my Father's house (all of Infinite, Intelligent, Creative Love's countless realms of progression) are many mansions (many vast areas of opportunity for progression in each realm.) If it were not so, I (Jesus) would have told you. I go to prepare a place for you (according to your soul progression)." (John 14:2)

After the Master demonstrated the Will of Infinite, Intelligent, Creative Love upon Earth-Eden, his soul went to prepare a place for souls to dwell once they have progressed through Creative

Consciousness into higher understanding, needing to reincarnate no more, ending Karma (cause and effect) and entering Grace (trust in Infinite, Intelligent Truth.)

A specific place is prepared for each and every one of you upon Earth-Eden according to *your deeds*! Remember, heaven, purgatory and hell are found in the Second Realm just as they are found on the First Realm (Earth-Eden). There are various places of opportunity for progression according to each soul's growth. Creative Love does not place you there, *you* do, through the free will of your own thoughts, words and deeds. Progress in Creative Consciousness to be in the place of high soul progression.

"Trust in the Lord (Infinite Intelligence) with all thine heart, and lean not unto thine own insight. In all thy ways acknowledge Him (Creative Love) and He (the only source) shall direct thy paths." (Prov. 3:5-6)

By praying silently to Creative Love you acknowledge Creative Love's existence, you establish communion, you begin to trust and you slowly but surely progress by following the ways of kindness, compassion, honesty, justice, respect and equality. All too often when one feels that one can "do it alone," or "doesn't need any help" when problems exist, the results are not the best because personal insight without Creative Consciousness is very limited and more than often exceedingly unstable. Trust in Creative Love which created your soul, which Loves you unconditionally. What have you got to lose? *Your soul!* What have you got to gain? *Everything!* The more you acknowledge, the more you trust. The more you trust, the more you follow Creative Love's Paths. The more you follow Creative Love's Paths, the more you reflect Creative Love to others, for you can only reflect to others what you yourself have acquired.

"God (Infinite, Intelligent, Creative Love) is our refuge and strength, a very present help in time of trouble." (Ps. 46:1)

Creative Love is your *only* source of all life, all strength, all hope, all protection and all love. Refuge and strength is Infinite

Intelligence! For is this not the Creative Love of *all* of which we are speaking? Is Creative Love not *always* present everywhere, not only in times of joy and happiness but also in times of trial, need, trouble and loneliness? Are not the times of joy, happiness, trial, need, trouble and loneliness upon Earth-Eden of your own making because of your kindness, compassion, honesty, justice and equality or because of your selfishness, non-concern, cheating and greed? Of course, by now you have learned that the priceless gift of free will which Creative Love has given to each of you can either progress or regress your soul. A variety of tools for life lies before you, and it is up to you as to what you shall build with these priceless tools of free will.

Infinite Intelligence is ever present to strengthen and comfort you, if you but realize this *fact* and understand that it works two ways: first, through the unfailing trust which Creative Love has in you, and second, through the unfailing trust which you *can* demonstrate in Creative Love as did the Example and Pathshower Jesus.

"In the world (the materialistic First Realm of Earth-Eden) ye shall have tribulation (regression): but be of good cheer; I (Jesus) have overcome the world (regression)." (John 16:33)

These are the words which John the Beloved, young companion of Jesus, recorded Jesus' telling his disciples: that in following Creative Consciousness and doing the Will of Infinite Intelligence, regression can be overcome. His hour had come in that he would soon conquer the flesh (the physical) and his work in this last incarnation would be finished. He tells of trials and tribulations which exist in the physical flesh due to the misuse of free will. He also tells you to be of good cheer and rejoice for when each of you places more value on the spiritual, the kindness, the compassion, the honesty, the justice, the respect, the equality with which you relate to friends, strangers and enemies will help you progress out of Karma (cause and effect) and enter Grace (Principal's highest Law).

As the Pathshower overcame through the giving up of "self" so *can* each of you follow his example and do likewise, for if you do not, what do *you* think will be the result??

"He (those) that saith he (they) is (are) in the light (enlightenment) and hateth his brother (others), is (are) in darkness (false self-righteousness) even until now. He (those) that loveth his brother (others) abideth in the light (enlightenment), and there is none occasion of stumbling (regression) in him (them)." (1 John 2 1:9-10)

We have stated many times before that *everyone* is your sister and brother, for all are related as offspring of Creative Love. Not necessarily related in the flesh, although many of you are in each incarnation and many of you are from previous incarnations, but mainly because you *all* were created as spiritual souls, therefore, you *all* are one. Relatives, friends, strangers and enemies, you all are each other's keepers. You must be concerned about each other, for if you are not, what kind of regression are you building upon Earth-Eden?

How *dare* you *defile* Infinite Intelligence which made you, gave you life, gave you free will! How *dare* you be so selfish as not to live in the ways of Creative Love and *hate* a brother, sister, husband, wife, mother, father, son, daughter, cousins, inlaws or *anyone*? You know that by hating you build up regressive Karma, which you *must* work off by meeting self. You know that when you pass through the shadow of the change called death, you can take nothing physical with you, except that *you* will take the Akashic records of your thoughts, words and deeds with you. Do you wish to be bogged down with hatred as burdensome luggage, or would you rather travel en-light-endly upon the path of Creative Joy and Love?

Put aside hatred, greed and self by meeting your shortcomings *now* and progressing upon the *only* path worth traveling, namely kindness, compassion, honesty, justice, respect, and equality. Try to understand the immensity and the infinity of Creative Love which is constantly present and wrapped lovingly around you for you to share with others.

"When thou prayest (commune in your heart with Creative Love), enter into thy closet (be alone), and when thou hast shut thy door (closed out the physical), pray to thy Father (Creative Love) which is in secret, and thy Father (Creative Love) which seeth in secret shall reward thee openly (or secretly)." (Matt. 6:6)

Prayer is one of the highest forms of soul progression when it is understood and performed properly. Communing in prayer is not telling Infinite Intelligence how to run Creation, is not bargaining with Infinite Intelligence; communing in prayer is not vain, boring repetition. "When you pray do *not* be like the hypocrites who pray aloud in public, raising their arms, beating their breasts, who think they are heard for their many words." (Matt. 6:5) Rather, when you commune, speak sincerely from your heart to Creative Love. Communing is praising and thanking Creative Love for all which has been given to you. It is actually speaking to God! But you know that! But do you *really* know that? Imagine if you had progressed enough to spiritually see God?? *Imagine!* It is in this manner of thought in which you should commune. Speak to Creative Love from your heart. Just as the Master closed the door to keep out any doubters or any disturbance when he resurrected anyone, so you should commune, *alone, silently* within your heart. Commune with the Love of love, the Kindness of kindness, the Compassion of compassion, the Honesty of honesty, the Justice of justice, the Respect of respect, the Equality of equality.

The closet of which the Master spoke is a little room, a chapel, a physical place to bar the non-progressiveness of Earth-Eden from the communer's mind. When you commune, begin to use the example of the Master as he used Creative Consciousness. Set aside a special place (when possible) in which to commune daily and privately at the same time (when possible). This manner of communication helps to establish a habit, a pattern of comfortableness. Eventually, when you feel freer in speaking to Creative Love and are able to block out physical distractions, you will find that you will be able to commune anywhere, and eventually you will begin to "live" a prayer as the Master taught all to pray "constantly."

When you commune alone (in secret) or silently in a crowd as you walk along performing your daily tasks, Creative Love always hears, *always* answers (rewards) when you are in a crowd (openly) or when you are alone (secretly). The hour or place for answer (reward) does vary according to Infinite, Intelligent, Wisdom.

"When Jesus came into the coasts of Caesarea of Phillippi, He asked His disciples saying,'Whom do men (people) say that I the son of Man (this reincarnated physical entity known as Jesus) am?' And they said, 'Some say that thou art John the Baptist; some, Elias; and others, Jeremiah, or one of the prophets (proving their belief in reincarnation).' He saith unto them, 'But whom say ye that I am?' And Simon Peter (who would later deny Jesus three times) answered and said, 'Thou art the Christ (the perfect human who rose above self to be at-one with Infinite Intelligence), the Son of the living God (a perfect child of Creative Love, the example for all souls upon Earth-Eden to follow in order to return to Infinite Intelligence).' And Jesus answered and said unto him, 'Blessed are thou, Simon Barjona (Peter); for flesh and blood hath not revealed it unto thee, but My Father (Infinite, Intelligent, Creative Love) which is in heaven (perfect harmony, perfect compassion, perfect justice).

And I say also unto thee, that thou art Peter (you Simon through presently thinking in Creative Consciousness are as a rock, "petre," speaking a foundational truth), and upon this rock (this truth, this manner of thinking, speaking and acting in Creative Consciousness) I (the Pathshower, the follower in the example of the *I Am*) will build my church (the temple-church, consisting of the physical body containing Creative Consciousness); and the gates of hell (anti-Creative Consciousness, the denial, the lie) shall not prevail against it. And I will give unto thee the keys of the Kingdom of Heaven (the teachings of Infinite Intelligence) and whatsoever thou (all souls upon Earth-Eden) shalt bind on Earth shall be bound in heaven; and whatsoever thou (all souls upon Earth-Eden) shalt loose on Earth shall be loosed in heaven (whatever grudges and sins which you do not forgive upon Earth-Eden, you shall carry into the Second Realm; therefore, let go of your animosities *now*!)'." (Matt. 16:13-19)

Let us emphatically say to you that it is Creative Consciousness which gave Simon Peter the insight to understand Jesus' demonstration of Creative Consciousness upon which the church is founded. *The church is founded upon Creative, Conscious, Infinite, Intelligent Love; not* upon any so-called direct succession of a follower of the Pathshower in grand display as an infallible leader, an emperor or a Caesar, but upon the Pathshower's demonstration of Creative Consciousness is the church built. "Render unto Caesar that which is Caesar's and unto God that which is God's" (Mark 12:17), taught the Master. There is nothing to render to Caesar because all is from and of God. This is further verified by Paul's letter to the early Christians in Corinth when he wrote: "For other foundation can no man (no one) lay than that is laid, which is Jesus Christ" (the foundation of the Creative Consciousness) (1 Cor. 3:11).

A person in the position of a religious leader in itself means *fallibility*. It is the individual soul which seeks to elevate itself to thinking and speaking in Creative Consciousness which is of importance. As Paul wrote to the Galileans: "There is neither Jew nor Greek, there is neither bond nor free, there is neither male nor female; for ye are all one in Christ Jesus (In Creative Consciousness)." (Gal 3:28)

The church triumphant is the church of Creative Consciousness taught by the Teacher of teachers and not the church of any over-structured system!! Matthew records early in his gospel the Master saying: "Whosoever hereath these sayings of mine and *doeth* these, I will liken him (them) unto a wise man (an intelligent individual), which built his (their) house (life) upon a rock (Creative Consciousness). And the rain (anti-Creative Consciousness) came, and the winds (the false ideas) blew and beat upon that house (that person) and it fell not (to wrong ideas, words and actions) for it was founded upon a rock (Creative Consciousness)." (Matt. 7:24-25)

The Teacher of teachers was steadfast in his teachings in that the rock of foundation for each soul's progression, as that of the church, is founded upon Creative Consciousness and the Pathshower, and not upon anything or anyone else.

"No man (person) hath ascended up to heaven, but he (they) that came down from Heaven, *even* the Son of Man which is in Heaven." (John 3:13)

These are the words recorded in John of Jesus' speaking to Nicodemus. Earlier in that chapter Jesus questions Nicodemus with "If I have told you earthly things and you believe not, how shall you believe if I tell you heavenly things?" (John 3:12) He was referring to the explanation which he had given Nicodemus concerning reincarnation. He said, "Except a man be born again, he cannot see the Kingdom of God" (John 3:3) and Nicodemus thought he had to re-enter his mother's womb! But the Master said a person must be born of water and spirit. This means a daily spiritual rebirth, a daily mental cleansing to obtain Creative Consciousness and *also* that as stated in John (3:13) (our title verse) "No person hath ascended up to heaven but that he (they) came down from Heaven, *even* the Son of Man (Jesus) which is in Heaven."

Each soul who entered Earth-Eden came *from Heaven* (Creative Love) and they (their soul) ascended from Earth-Eden to higher realms after the change called death. After a period of time the soul or spirit reincarnates, is born again upon Earth-Eden in the flesh (the water sac which surrounds the fetus and breaks at birth) thus the person is reborn of "spirit" and "water." This is to further work off Karma and eventually enter Grace through Creative Consciousness *even* as the Son of Man had to do in order to obtain Heaven (the at-one-ment with Infinite Intelligence) or in other words: "Being made perfect (in Creative Consciousness) as Infinite Love is perfect." Heaven is perfect harmony with Infinite Love and at this point the Master was in harmony with Infinite Love, thus was "in Heaven" (Matt. 5:48).

The ritualistic physical baptism by John the Baptist was simply an outward sign for those of low soul progression (that which was born of the flesh), to learn from as a first step in understanding Creative Consciousness, eventually not needing a physical baptism, but having a spiritual cleansing (that which is born of the spirit)!

Remember the purpose of this textbook is "to set the record straight." We are as one voice crying to Earth-Eden, trying to prevent a wilderness (Matt. 3:3). *Value* your present days upon Earth-Eden. Follow the eleventh commandment: "Thou shalt not waste." Time is a precious commodity. Waste it not, waste not your present incarnation, follow the teachings of the Pathshower for your soul progression in kindness, compassion, honesty, justice, respect and equality. You *know* "earthly things," now *know* "Heavenly things!!"

"Judge not, that you be not judged. For with what judgment you judge, you shall be judged; and with that measure you mete, it shall be measured unto you again." (Matt. 7:1-2)

These are the words recorded in Matthew's gospel as being spoken by the Master in his "Sermon on the Mount." As we have stated before, we are writing this book in order to "set the record straight." Much misunderstanding has arisen over this quotation throughout the centuries because of the absence of one word. The message which the Master was teaching was this: "Judge not *unrighteously,* so that you be not judged *unrighteously*. For with what judgment you judge, you shall be judged, and with what measure you mete, it shall be measured to you again."

This is the teaching of the second highest law of Karma, which automatically goes into effect when the highest Law of Grace is rejected or not practiced. The Master went on to explain how Karma *can* be overcome, and how Grace can be entered into. "Ask (for Creative Consciousness) and it shall be given you; seek (Creative Consciousness) and you shall find (it); knock and it (Creative Consciousness) shall be opened unto you; for everyone that asketh (for Creative Consciousness) receiveth; and they who seeketh (Creative Consciousness) findeth; and to those who knocketh; it (Creative Consciousness) shall be opened (revealed)" (Matt. 7:7-8).

The Master also warns that: "Not every one that saith unto me 'Lord, Lord' shall enter into the Kingdom of Heaven (the state of righteousness); but those who do the Will of my Father (Infinite, Intelligent, Creative Love) which is in heaven (is perfect righteousness in perfect righteousness). Many will say to Me that day, Lord, Lord, have we not prophesied in Thy Name? And in Thy Name cast out devils? And in Thy name done many wonderful works? And then I will profess to them, I never knew you, (iniquity is not known to Infinite, Intelligent, Creative Love or to those who demonstrate its Perfect Will), depart from me, you that work iniquity (until you have entered Grace through Creative Consciousness by doing works of kindness, compassion, honesty, justice, respect and equality, and have left the tethers of Karma having your own acts of unrighteous *self* measured to you again and again, time after time, reincarnation after reincarnation. *Judge not unrighteously*)" (Matt. 7:21-23)!

"If you continue (progress) in my (Jesus') word (example) then you are my (Jesus') disciples, and you *shall know the truth* (Infinite Intelligence), and the *truth shall* make you free (from self, from Karma to enter Grace)." (John 8:31,32)

For your own sake, listen to these soul-progressive words of your teacher-example, which the beloved John records! You *shall* find and know the "Truth" in Creative Consciousness *when you demonstrate lovingly* in your present incarnation upon Earth-Eden the Will (kindness, compassion, honesty, justice and equality) of Infinite, Intelligent, Creative Love as did the Pathshower, your ever-Creative Example.

Truth is the eternal principle which is Infinite, Intelligent, Creative Love. It is that principle which governs all that is. For Infinite, Intelligent, Creative Love created you in the reflective image of that principle. With the free will given to each living soul by Creative Love, you can return to the Principle of Truth, therefore, by small yet constant steps begin your journey homeward, heavenward. The admitting to yourself of your goal to let go of the nothingness of greed, want and desire to be replaced by sharing, kindness, and compassion is knowing the Truth, and is the beginning of being made free from all shackles and tethers of regression and nothingness.

In your deepest thoughts, in your most secret knowledge, you *know* what the Truth of life is. Go regularly to the temple of your heart, meet with Creative Love and feel the free-soaring experience of every *truthful* soul in its journey to reunite with Infinite Intelligence, in its journey to be no longer earth-bound, in its journey to become at-one with all creation in metaphysical, spiritual Grace. As you enter deeper in Love's Graceful Way of Life, you become more truthful with yourself, with others and with Creative Love. Thus you become more free—free from regression, free from sickness and eventually free from the change called death, needing to reincarnate *no more*. Soar for the ethereal. Soar for the Truth.

"For as in Adam all die (spiritually), so also in Christ all shall be made alive (spiritually)."(1 Cor. 15:22)

This death is not of the physical nature, rather of the spiritual. Adam and Eve (soul mates) who, being created in the image of Infinite, Intelligent, Creative Love, did indeed live so upon Earth-Eden until, through free will, they decided not to follow the Will of Infinite, Intelligent, Creative Love and died spiritually. Then eons later, after many reincarnations, the soul of the entity known as Jesus re-entered upon Earth-Eden and demonstrated perfect obedience to Infinite Intelligence through Creative Consciousness. It was this Jesus Who became the Pathshower for *all* souls upon Earth-Eden. Why Jesus? Because the soul of the Christ through its many reincarnations upon Earth-Eden always progressed in Creative Consciousness higher and higher, as did the souls of Mary and Joseph. By the complete overcoming of self (the adam or spiritual death), the result was eternal spiritual Life through Creative Consciousness.

"And Mary said (to the Angel) 'Behold the handmaid (servant) of the Lord (Infinite, Intelligent, Creative Love); be it done unto me according to Thy Word (Principal Law). And the angel (one of those among you) departed from her." (Luke 1:38)

If all of you upon Earth-Eden would only follow the immaculate example of Creative Consciousness which Mary and Joseph demonstrated in obeying Creative Love's Will!! Each and every one of you souls in the flesh today can be handmaids or servants of kindness, compassion, honesty, justice, respect, and equality, for angel-thoughts communing with you from "those among you" are of great soul progressive value. Meditate, speak to Creative Love, then listen for answers. Once this has become a habit you may be greatly surprised as to whom your angels are.

"He (anyone who leads (others) into captivity (preventing their soul progression), shall go into captivity (shall become slaves of 'self,' 'selfishness'). He (anyone) who kills with the sword shall be killed with the sword." (Rev. 13:10)

"Then said Jesus to him (one of his apostles in the Garden of Gethsemane), 'Put away your sword. For anyone who takes the sword (kills by the sword), shall perish by the sword (shall themselves die by the sword).'" (Matt. 26:52)

"You have heard it said, 'An eye for an eye and a tooth for a tooth; but I (Jesus teaching Creative Consciousness) say unto you, resist no one who is evil (flee not from them, but demonstrate to them Creative Consciousness); but whosoever strikes you on your right cheek, turn to them the other cheek also.' You have heard it said 'You shall love your neighbor and hate your enemy' but I (Jesus teaching Creative Consciousness) say to you, `Love your enemies, bless those who curse you, do good to those who hate you and pray for those who despitefully use and persecute you.'" (Matt. 5:38, 39, 43, 44)

The first scripture (Rev. 13:10) states the Second highest Law of Karma. Now we know that this statement is simply not true if one lives but one life upon Earth-Eden. We *also* know that reincarnation *does* exist. Therefore, here once more is scriptural proof of reincarnation. If an entity has murdered someone in one of their previous incarnations they shall in the present or in a future incarnation die by being killed through the law of Karma (cause and effect) unless that individual has an exceedingly progressive incarnation rising above "self," leaving Karma, entering Grace, having to reincarnate no more, therefore, not needing to die by the sword.

This holds true for any non-progressive or wanton act. If you falsely aid in the imprisonment of an innocent entity the same shall happen to you in the present or in some future incarnation unless you soulfully progress through kindness, compassion, honesty, justice, respect and equality to such a height as to enter Grace.

The second scripture (Matt. 26:52) quotes the Master reinforcing that second highest Law of Karma. He tells one of his apostles to put away their sword for they were not following his teachings of forgiveness, or the highest Law of Grace.

The third scripture, (Matt. 5:38,39,43,44) quotes the Master reinforcing the highest Law of Grace in teaching them to love their enemies, thus leaving the second highest Law of Karma by demonstrating Creative Consciousness and entering Grace as he did.

"Where your treasure is, there your heart is also." (Matt. 6:21)

We feel this is quite self-explanatory but do ask you to read it again and then ponder truthfully upon it. Where is your heart?

"He (Infinite, Intelligent, Creative Love) makes the sun to rise upon the evil and the good, and sends rain upon the just and the unjust." (Matt. 5:45)

The metaphysical enlightenment of this profound truth taught by the Master through Creative Consciousness in his Sermon on the Mount, is proof of Creative Love's constant gift of free will given to you souls in the flesh upon Earth-Eden. This gift, as all gifts of opportunity of soul progression, is also proof of Creative Love's constant forgiveness to each and every one of you, with constant opportunity to overcome Karma, enter Grace and need to go out no more (reincarnate no more).

The sunlight of warm soulful enlightenment and the cleansing rain of the refreshing, soulful-quenching thirst for righteousness is given with Hopeful Love by Creative Love which comforts and protects as a mother or father comforts and protects unswervingly.

"As one whom his mother comforted, so shall I (Infinite, Intelligent, Creative Love) comfort you." (Isa. 66:13)

This is a sacred promise of Creative Love for all souls throughout all ages. You upon Earth-Eden are not alone. Creative Love is your constant Comforter in thought, in manner, in Spirit of Holiness. The Master reminded his apostles that they would not be left as orphans when he would be gone, but that a Comforter, a Spirit of Holy Concerned Love (which is the essence of Love) would be with them (John 14:18). Not that it *had ever left Earth-Eden*! They simply needed reminding of it at that time, as you upon Earth-Eden need reminding now and again that you have a Comforter which is Infinite Intelligence. This Creative Love never stops watching over *all* of creation continually, including *you*!!

"From Zion (the *only* Source, the Realm of Creative Love) shall go forth instruction and the word (Jesus teaching Creative Conscious Truth) of the Lord (Infinite Intelligence) from Jerusalem (and Jesus did!). He (Infinite Intelligence) shall judge between the nations (justly, righteously) and impose terms on many people (all who have not progressed to the state of Grace and shall constantly give opportunity for collective soul progression, even though it may seem as punishment to some nations, for it may be the only or the best way for them to progress). They (those of high soul progression in Creative Consciousness) shall beat their swords into plowshares and their spears into pruning hooks (shall beat not only their physical weapons into tools of progression but shall also turn their verbal spears of the tongue into pruning hooks to verbally curb untruths, gossip and self praise.) One nation shall not raise the sword (weapons and unjust politics) against another (their sisters and brothers) nor shall they train for war again (nor shall even the thought enter their minds.)" (Isa. 2:3-4)

Not only is this found upon the Third Realm and higher realms, but it can occasionally be found on the Second Realm and *is possible upon Earth-Eden* if only you would strive to eliminate the root regression of self through selflessness and replace it with care, concern and love for friend, stranger and enemy.

Realize that you *are being watched*, you upon Earth-Eden! Realize that you *are being loved* by Creative Love; the Love which comforts and protects as a mother and father comforts and protects unswervingly! You *can* turn Earth into Eden! You *can* beat your swords into plowshares and your spears into pruning hooks!
You can! You must!

"If today (now is the day of salvation) you hear His (Infinite,

Intelligence) voice (that still small voice within), harden not your hearts (*listen*)." (Ps. 95:7-8)

Turn not away from the invitation of Infinite Intelligence. Follow the path of kindness, compassion, honesty, justice, respect, and equality, then by small yet constant steps ascend the staircase of progressive ways which lead you home (heavenward), needing to return no more (reincarnate no more), rather being at-one with Creative Love.

"Verily (in Truth) I (Jesus teaching Creative Consciousness) say unto you (the chief priests and elders of the people in the temple), that the publicans (tax collectors) and the harlots (prostitutes) shall march into the kingdom of God before you." (Matt. 21: 31)

Why? Because many a prostitute and tax collector had more kindness, compassion, honesty, justice, respect, and equality in their thoughts, words and deeds than the leaders and followers of some overstructured religions. Remember, the Pathshower in demonstrating the Creative Way was able to look into their hearts, for he and the Almighty were as one in Creative Consciousness. What is in your heart?

"Sacrifice or oblation you (Infinite Intelligence) do not desire, rather ears open to obedience to do Your Will." (Ps. 40:6)

All too often living souls in the flesh have the false notion that sacrifice is a stepping stone towards salvation. *Wrong!* Soul progression is better attained as Principal requested, that in doing the Will of Infinite, Intelligent, Creative Love and that Will, that Love, that Request, that Loving Guidance is kindness, compassion, honesty, justice and equality, for yourself and *all* others. If this seems as an offering to you, if kindness, compassion, honesty, justice, respect, justice and equality seem an oblation, then look deeply into your heart and ask yourself this question (for these offenses will truly sacrifice your soul progression): "What is *not* sacrifice: cruelty, non-caring, lies and injustice?"

Believe us from the Third Realm as we cry to you in one voice through our channeling-instrument Curt, you upon the First Realm known as Earth-Eden, that mental and physical wilderness: "*The more you try to follow the ways of Infinite, Intelligent, Creative Love, the easier it becomes, the freer you become, the more truthful you become, thus the truth of doing Creative Love's Will shall make you free from self-enslavement ." We have learned this lesson; so can you!*

"Give thanks to the Lord (Infinite, Intelligent, Creative Love), worship (live according to Principal) in holy attire (in Creative Conscious thoughts, words and deeds)." (Ps 29:1-2)

The only *valid* way in which you can truly show your thankfulness is to array yourself, to attire yourself, to clothe yourself with kindness, compassion, honesty, justice, respect, and equality. As we have stated earlier, there is only one message and we constantly point it out to you throughout the scriptures. Seek the metaphysical wisdom throughout the scriptures, which is the *only* message we are trying to impress upon you in the living flesh as have many of "those among you" throughout the ages. Progress your planet collectively with your *individual* soul progression through *kindness, compassion, honesty, justice, respect and equality.*

"I (Jesus the Master Pathshower teaching Truth in Creative Consciousness) say unto you (all living souls in the flesh upon Earth-Eden), 'Ask (for guidance in soul progression) and it shall be given to you, seek (the ways of Infinite, Intelligent, Creative Love) and you shall find (that path), knock (on the door of the hall of the spiritual Akashic Records of your past incarnations) and it shall be opened to you, for everyone who asks will receive, everyone who seeks will find, and to everyone who knocks, it will be opened.'" (Luke 11:9)

Self explanatory. Re-read the Bible Progression which starts on page 187, line 8, and goes through page 188, line 4.

"Therefore I (Jesus) speak to them (the unenlightened crowds) in parables (simply worded stories demonstrating soul progression) because they, seeing, see not (Creative Conscious Progression); and hearing, they hear not (Creative Conscious Progression); neither do they understand (Creative Conscious Progression)." (Matt. 13:13)

Self explanatory.

"You who are in the flesh (entities upon Earth-Eden who think with materialistic consciousness) cannot please God (cannot presently be perfect as Infinite, Intelligent, Creative Love wishes you to be), but you (those of you who follow in thought, word and deed the teachings of the Pathshower) who are not in the flesh (not materialistic minded); but (progressing) in the Spirit (the spirit of the Master's teachings), since the Spirit of God (Infinite, Intelligent, Creative Love) dwells in you." (Rom. 8:8-9)

Self explanatory.

"Jesus said to the crowd: 'The reign of God is like a buried treasure'." (Matt. 13:44)

The Kingdom of heaven is within. Heaven (Grace), the state of following the harmonious, soul-progressive ways of Infinite, Intelligent, Creative Love, *is* the buried treasure. It is Creative Consciousness within each and every living soul upon Earth-Eden and *can* be demonstrated as the Pathshower demonstrated. He said, "My yoke is easy, and my burden is light," (Matt. 11:30) and it becomes lighter as the enlightenment becomes clearer by small yet constant steps as one ascends the staircase of kindness, compassion, honesty, justice, respect, and equality.

Infinite, Intelligent, Creative, Loving Law is a treasure more precious than thousands of pieces of silver or gold. To follow the Law of Infinite, Intelligent, Creative Love through Creative Consciousness is a comfort and delight giving constant understanding and soul progression to the simple and the wise.

The kingdom *has* come, is presently here upon Earth-Eden in the degree it is *demonstrated by you*. You *have* the ability, you have the constant supply of Creative Love. The kingdom, the reign of heavenly peace *is* the priceless treasure within you. It is yours for the taking.

What a gift!

"Wrath and anger are hateful things, yet the sinner (regressor) hugs them tightly. The vengeful will suffer the Lord's vengeance (Karma, reaping what they have sown because they rejected Grace, rejected doing the Will of Infinite, Intelligent, Creative Love), for he (the Law of Karma) remembers their sins (regressions) in detail (every dot and comma). Forgive your neighbors' injustice (towards you, others and the regressor); then when you pray (silently, alone, communing with Creative Love) your own sins (regressions) will be forgiven (by Creative Love and yourself, leaving soul regression and beginning soul progression).

Should a man (any soul upon Earth-Eden) nourish anger against his (their) fellows (anyone) and expect healing (soul progression) from the Lord (escape the justice of Karma)? Should a man (any soul upon Earth-Eden) refuse mercy to his (their) fellows (anyone), yet seek pardon for his (their) own sins (regressions)? If he (anyone) who is but flesh (souls upon Earth-Eden) cherishes wrath (severe soul regression), who will forgive his (their) sins? (Very few upon Earth-Eden, but the road to forgiveness is constantly kept open by Infinite, Intelligent, Creative Love if the regressor but chooses to take it.) Remember your last days (the last time you were regressive,) set enmity aside, remember death (the flesh does not live eternally, the soul does) and decay (spiritual regression) and cease from sin (regression)! Think of the commandments (Principal), hate not your neighbor (All are your neighbors), overlook faults (of others)." (Sirach 27:30 & 28:1-7)

We wish to point out an exceedingly important fact concerning this verse. This was written hundreds of years before the Master entered Earth-Eden, yet here as with Elijah (when Elijah demonstrated Creative Consciousness in resurrecting the little boy) one can find Creative Conscious teachings of Infinite, Intelligent, Creative Love as stated in Sirach: "Think of the commandments, hate not your neighbor," then the Master later embellished upon this when he taught: "The greatest commandment is to love your God with all your heart, soul, and mind, and the second is like unto it, to love your neighbor as yourself." (Matt. 22:37).

These Creative Consciousness teachings are still in effect today. It is the Law of Grace which leads the path upward away from the Law of Karma.

"Then came Peter to Him (Jesus), and said, 'Lord, how often shall my brother (anyone) sin (regress) against me, and I forgive him (them)? Till seven times?' Jesus said unto him (Peter), 'I say not unto you until seven times; but until seventy times seven (always).' Therefore is the kingdom of heaven (total paradise in living Creative Consciousness) likened unto a certain king, who would take account of his servants. And when he had begun to reckon (balance his accounts), one was brought to him who owed him ten thousand talents (large amounts of silver). But forasmuch as he had not paid, his lord (the king) commanded him to be sold, and his wife, and children, and all that he had, and payment to be made. The servant therefore fell down and worshipped him saying, 'Lord (king) have patience with me and I will pay you all which I owe.' Then the lord (the king) of that servant was moved with compassion, released him and forgave him the debt.

But the same servant went out and found one of his fellow-servants who owed him one hundred pence (a very small amount) and he laid his hands on him and took him by the throat saying: 'Pay me what you owe me!' And his fellow-servant fell down at his feet and besought him saying: 'Have patience with me and I will repay you all.' But he (the king's forgiven servant) would not relent, and cast him (his fellow-servant) into prison, till he should pay the debt.

So when the other fellow-servants saw what had happened, they were very sorry (and upset), and came and told their lord (the king) all that had happened. Then his lord (the king) called him and said to him: 'Oh you wicked servant, I forgave you all your debt (*Grace*), because you begged me to do so. Should you not also have had compassion on your fellow-servant even as I had pity on you (also have demonstrated *Grace*)?' And his lord (the king) was wroth (bitterly angry) and delivered him to the tormentors, till he should pay *all* that was due unto him (*Karma*, cause and effect, after rejecting Grace, having to reap what was sown). So likewise shall My heavenly Father, (not Infinite, Intelligent, Creative Love, rather *Karma*) do also unto you, if you from your hearts forgive not every one his brother (*anyone*) their trespasses (wrongs)." (Matt. 18:21-35)

Here we find the Teacher of teachers teaching in Creative Consciousness, the manner in which the Second Highest Law of Karma (cause and effect) automatically is enforced if the Highest Law of Grace is not demonstrated. We would suggest that you re-read Chapter 9 of Forgiveness Progression to familiarize yourself with Creative Love's ways of constantly bringing all souls in the flesh upon Earth-Eden to higher soul progression. Although Karma may seem severe, *it is your choice. You can demonstrate forgiveness instead.*

"Come unto me, all you that labor (work toward soul progression) and are heavy laden (with guilt, regression and problems), and I (the Pathshower demonstrating the teachings of Creative Consciousness) will give you rest (a time for reflection, re-evaluation and gathering of spiritual and physical energies). Take my yoke (the teaching and demonstrating of Creative Love's Ways through Creative Consciousness) upon *you*, and learn from me; for I (Creative Conscious strength within me) am (is) meek and lowly (not proudly puffed-up) in heart; and you shall find rest (serene peace) unto your souls. For my *yoke* is easy (not as the yoke of enslaved servants or tethered beasts of burden) and my burden (the task of bringing Creative Consciousness to souls in the flesh upon Earth-Eden) is light (not heavy because of spiritual enlightenment)." (Matt. 12:28-30)

Whatever seemingly heavy burden you carry upon your shoulders of life can be lightened through thinking, speaking and demonstrating Creative Consciousness. Remember, *your problems are of your own making. Let go of non-progressive thoughts, words, and deeds. forgive, let go, and your burdens will become lighter and lighter in demonstrating creative ways. Try it. It Works.*

"The Word (the Pathshower, demonstrating the Truth of Infinite, Intelligent, Creative Love through Creative Consciousness) was made flesh (incarnated) and dwelt among us (upon Earth-Eden for a short period of time)." (John 1:14)

The Word, the Truth, the Creativity, are all one in that they are the Way for *all* upon Earth-Eden to live *the life* of soul progression as did the Master who demonstrated Creative Love's kindness, compassion, honesty, justice, respect, and equality.

"Store not up for yourselves treasures (greed, falsely thought of as treasures) upon earth where moth and rust do corrupt (destroy) and where thieves break in and steal; rather store up for yourself (and others) treasures (spiritual deeds, mitzvahs) in heaven (in Infinite, Intelligent, Loving Harmony) where neither moth nor rust do corrupt (destroy), and where thieves do not break in and steal." (Matt. 6:19, 20)

Self explanatory.

"Dismiss all anxiety from your minds (needless energy drain). Present your needs to God (Infinite, Intelligent, Creative Love) in every form of prayer and in petitions full of gratitude (in thought, word and deed). Then God's own Peace (Perfect Peace of perfect peace) which is beyond all understanding (only presently), will stand guard over your hearts and minds in Christ Jesus (in the Pathshower's teachings of Creative Consciousness for you to follow)." (Phil. 4:6-7)

Self explanatory.

"Create in me a clean heart, O God, and renew a right spirit within me. Cast me not away from Your presence, and take not Your holy spirit from me. Restore unto me the joy of Your salvation, and uphold me with Your free spirit." (Ps. 51:10-12)

As we have stated before, we channel these sessions with the purpose of "setting the record straight." Here in this often familiar psalm it foolishly begs Infinite Intelligence to do your soul progression for you. Creative Love *has* created you with a clean heart! You *constantly* have the opportunities to renew a Creative Conscious, righteous spirit within you! Infinite, Intelligent, Creative Love *never* casts you away, rather it is you living souls in the flesh upon Earth-Eden who, through selfish use of your free will, separate yourselves from the Love's Ways. The Spirit of Holiness will never be taken from you, rather it is *constantly* there for your progression if you but choose to use it. Then and only then will the joy of salvation be restored to you by your own *obedience* when you truly uphold the free spirit of doing Love's Will unto yourself and others in thought, word and deed through kindness, compassion, honesty, justice, respect and equality.

A wiser, more soul-progressive metaphysical translation of this psalm to meditate upon is as follows:

"Infinite, Intelligent, Creative Love has created me with a clean heart, and *constantly* gives me the opportunity to renew a Creative Conscious, righteous spirit within me. Infinite, Intelligent, Creative Love *never* casts anyone away. The Spirit of Holiness is *constantly* present for my progression if I but choose to use it. Then, and only then, will the joy of salvation be restored to me by my own *obedience* when I truly uphold the free spirit of doing Love's Will unto myself and others in thought, word and deed through kindness, compassion, honesty, justice, respect, and equality."

"You shall pray to Him (Infinite, Intelligent, Creative Love) and He (Infinite, Intelligent, Creative Love) *will* hear you, and you shall pay your vows (keep your promises of soul progression.) Then when you decree a thing (establish a goal in Creative Consciousness) it *will* be established to you and the light (soulful enlightenment) *will* shine (guide) upon your ways (your paths upon Earth-Eden.)" (Job 22:27-28)

It will be established to you! Decree, set goals, then exercise your birthright as a living, loving soul of Infinite Intelligence. It is that simple! It is that true! It is that progressive!

As it is proclaimed by the parable-character Job who represents the souls in the flesh upon Earth-Eden, you *can* establish *all* which is necessary for your soul progression but you must take the initiative to do so. You have the power to move mountains (spiritual

1 and physical), to destroy mountains (spiritual and physical), or to preserve mountains (spiritual and physical). Earth can be Edenized; it is up to you. Make this your objective!

Chapter 26
Objective Progression

Keep objectiveness in mind, flow in the power of Creative Consciousness, and you will soar to heights of progression which are limitless. Limits are negative barriers which you mentally place in your path of progression. *You* place the thoughts in your mind, therefore also realize that *you* can control your thoughts. Think beyond your present situation in life. See a mental picture of your progressive future as you trust it will be in your mind's eye and be prepared to achieve the objective.

See your present and your future through the eyes of Creative Consciousness as did the Pathshower. He became creative by always "seeing" the *truth* of Love's Will in even his most menial daily tasks of life upon Earth-Eden. His objectivity was the straight and narrow path of setting aside self through concern for others whether they were friends, strangers or enemies; thus broadening that path with trust in Infinite, Intelligent, Creative Love's Ways. This is done in the realization that the spiritual, positive flow of energy is limitless. Shake the negative dust from your feet and tread upon the path which leads to heights of spiritual positiveness. Your physical body shall return to dust but your spiritual soul shall continue after the change called death and the only thing which you will be able to take with you will be your recorded past! Begin *now* to grow with an objective mind flowing with progressive thoughts of Creative Consciousness.

The objectivity of Creative Consciousness was recorded by King Solomon in the Old Testament: "Wisdom (insight) is the principal thing (rule); therefore, get wisdom (insight) and with all your getting, get understanding (the realization that your insight comes from within, which is the source of Infinite, Intelligent, Creative Love)." (Prov. 4:7)

Insight is inner-sight, inner-wisdom, inner-understanding, inner-knowledge; that part of Infinite Intelligence which makes you at one with the cosmos, at one with creation, at one with Infinite Intelligence, at one with all others, at one with yourself, non-divided, *whole*. What is this insight, this inner energy? It is the spiritual manna, the energy of all life flowing from the only source, Infinite, Intelligent, Creative Love, saying: "If you open yourself to My Ways, *you will be* as *I Am*; if you do not open yourself to My ways, I will still continue to give you endless opportunities to do so, for *I* still *am*!"

Every burden can be turned into a blessing, in that it is an opportunity to grow in soul; as every so-called problem is a challenge which can be turned into a progression. Be thankful for the constant opportunities which Infinite, Intelligent, Creative Love gives you daily in order to eventually become perfect in kindness, compassion, honesty, justice, respect and equality as Love is Perfect.

Become more aware of your unity with all other living creatures, with all vegetation, with the minerals of Earth-Eden itself and with the liquids and gasses which surround it, for they are as *you*, all part of the handiwork of Creative Love. Become more aware of your place not only upon Earth-Eden but in the limitless cosmos itself. Become more aware of your *oneness* and *uniqueness* in all Creation. Become more aware of your purpose and your power as part of the constant progression of all creation. Then by small yet constant steps ascend the staircase of progression through at-one-ment for you already *have* the courage to do so! Where does this courage come from? From the *only* source, which is Infinite, Intelligent, Creative Love, and your portion is always there and *always* greater than your need!!

With this assurance of courage you can easily follow any progressive objective for yourself once you have set a firm foundation in Creative Consciousness; for Creative Consciousness is the ever-guiding light which eliminates all shadow of doubt. It illuminates your path of progression with assuredness, and thus enables you to reflect that attitude toward others, creating more mental and spiritual light in the cosmos. Remember, light reflects light, assuredness reflects assuredness, objectiveness reflects objectiveness.

You *can* achieve any of your progressive objectives. Set your sights on a specific goal of spiritual growth or physical endeavor, and by working with Creative Consciousness in the Principles of kindness, compassion, honesty, justice, respect and equality you *will* achieve your objective. *Know* that you will, and simply be prepared for the progressive results. "Ask (yourself to try), and you *shall* receive, knock (at the door of opportunity) and it *shall be opened*!" (Matt. 7:7). The more you try, the more you knock, the more doors of progression will open for you.

Seek and you *will* find the doors of objective progression. In Love's house are many mansions with many rooms, with many doors (John 14:2), *all* of which you are not only permitted to enter but constantly, lovingly being guided to enter for your objective, soulful progression. Do you still doubt your abilities? Then think of the countless blades of grass growing side by side in a vast field. Infinite, Intelligent, Creative Love created *each one* of them *knowingly*. They are *not* created by chance but by Love's objective, purposeful understanding. Think deeply for one moment; do you still have doubt of your abilities considering Who created you *knowingly, objectively, purposefully, understandingly, lovingly?!*

Set clear objectives for your future. Be realistic in thought and direct in action. Fear not to set foot and tread upon a new path, for as we have told you before, you travel not alone. Infinite, Intelligent, Creative Love is your constant staff and stay. Prepare with the positiveness of Creative Consciousness knowing that your only purpose upon Earth-Eden is to progress in soul and rejoicingly return home to be with the Loving Almighty and the ninety and nine (countless souls) who have not strayed from heaven (Luke 15:7). You can do it!!

Knock, and doors of opportunity *will* open for you when you work metaphysically with Creative Consciousness within you (Matt. 7:7). The doors through which you are to pass for your soul progression cannot and will not be closed for you if you but walk that straight and narrow path of the Pathshower Jesus which leads to those doors.

Ask for soul progression and you shall be given constant

opportunities to progress both spiritually and physically if your objective is soul-progressive. Your free will is the key which unlocks the tethering chains of stagnation.

Reason is the presiding motivation which culminates many of your daily activities; however, add metaphysical openness and parapsychological channeling to it, and you will make spiritual and material strides of fast and vast progression beyond any limited ideas which you may now have of your future. Soar for the empyreal. Your future will progress as you let go of mental doubts. Re-evaluate your spiritual treasury and then watch your financial treasury follow suit. Never be a slave to material want, for not all the gold of Ophir can save one soul, yet one single soul is worth more than all the gold and gems upon Earth-Eden (Job 28:16). Value your soul. Remember that Infinite, Intelligent, Creative Love loves you beyond your present comprehension. Soar for the empyreal of spiritual progression of your soul and all other needs will be given more than abundantly unto you.

It is the inner strength stored in your soul from Creative Love with which each of you upon Earth-Eden can easily draw in time of need, if you but take the time to sit down and meditate, thus releasing that spiritual, progressive energy. As it flows forth it cleanses as well as strengthens, thus washing away fears as well as doubts as it rejuvenates you. Sit down, be still and *know* from where your strength comes (Ps. 46:10)! Each of you has equal opportunity and access to this dynamic, endless supply of treasure! It is yours simply for the applying. It makes *all* rough places of your life smooth (Isa. 40:4). Know it!

Prevalence in any situation is a key factor of growth, be it spiritual or physical. Prevalence becomes easier to maintain as the entity practices it by small yet constant steps. As the entity progresses, the soul progresses and vice versa. Therefore, physical progression can aid spiritual progression and spiritual progression can aid physical progression.

Strength for prevalence can also be gained from your dreams. Remember your dreams, your daydreams, your ideas, your ideals from your earliest childhood and try to remember them as clearly as possible. This may take time but after several attempts through a one or two week period you can begin to remember more. Why is the remembrance of early youth's thoughts important? Because at the early stage of the incarnation of your soul into your present physical body the brain was not cluttered with many materialistic thoughts. It was clearer and closer to the pre-incarnation, thus closer to spiritual goals which are to aid the present entity in objective soul progression. Your thoughts were purer in kindness, compassion, honesty, justice, respect and equality, and therefore more soulfully objective. You were closer to the Second and Third Realms in thought at that time than at a later age.

Strive to remember your early goals and see how they can be of help to you now. See how close you have stayed, thus progressed, or how far you have strayed and are presently in need of corrective, objective progression. Separate the progressive wheat-thoughts from the non-progressive, weed-tare-thoughts and grow in objectiveness. You are *not* as putty in the hands of a whimsical deity, rather you are as the finest of clay created by Creative Love which has given you the objective free will to mold *yourself* in Love's image, to overcome many so-called obstacles such as fear of death, regression and sickness through objective Creative Conscious healing.

Chapter 27
Healing Progression

Perhaps the best way for us to begin this chapter is to point out that healing, be it spiritual or physical, is a manifestation which is sought to overturn another manifestation. That is to say that healing is a process of altering results of another process. Be it spiritual or physical it is a manifestation which will enable you to heal conditions you yourself have created in this incarnation because of lack, carelessness or greed, or it is a manifestation which will enable you to heal conditions which are the result of a past Karma (dealing with the same).

Search deeply within yourself and meditate for possible reasons for illness, injury or uncomfortableness. Give yourself direct verbal instructions before meditation to seek out the most suitable manner in which to heal yourself or others. Know that you all have the reflecting power of Infinite, Intelligent, Creative Love within each of you to constantly heal and make entirely whole.

Work alone or with a group to channel energy for healing on a regular basis. Work together weekly at the same hour in the same place if possible, just as you would for a meditative progression session.

As the medical profession uses preventive medicine in order to prevent illness, so can you use preventive meditation which will release healing energy to help keep body and soul on a non-illness, non-injury course.

Mental work combined with the laying on of hands can often create a spiritual and physical healing combination that can aid in the progression of healing, ever keeping in mind the healthy image in which Infinite, Intelligent, Creative Love created you.

Healing can also be manifested by meditating deeply with your head towards the north and your feet towards the south (reverse position if you live south of the equator) as you lie in bed just before going to sleep at night. Meditate upon the manifestation of the healing, then drift off into sleep with the thought that help will be given to you during sleep. This may require several days or several weeks of dedicated, disciplined practice to achieve; however remember it is by small yet constant steps that one ascends the staircase of the Creative Conscious art of healing. Blind faith cannot accomplish healing. However, *knowing that it is within your co-creative ability to do so can result in the truth of perfect progression known as healing. Perfect spiritual and physical manifestation can make each living soul in the flesh holy and whole.*

Through Creative Conscious thinking, think thoughts of holistic spiritual progression and "wholistic" physical progression. Natural quartz crystals, lapis lazuli, various gem stones, copper, gold, countless other metals and pyramids can be used as aids in metaphysical-healing depending upon the individual; however, these are merely aids for the beginner, as the progressed metaphysician does not need them to heal. The progressed metaphysician *knows* that the mind is ever the builder, ever the healer, as does the progressed medical doctor realize this fact. However, often for the patient's need of a kind touch, the laying on of hands can be of great benefit and nurturing comfort.

Be utmost thankful for the faithful ancient and modern medical physicians who through dedicated lives helped heal with medical and surgical procedures.

Be utmost thankful for the faithful ancient and modern homeopathic practitioners who through dedicated lives helped heal with holistic remedies.

Be utmost thankful for the faithful ancient and modern metaphysicians who through dedicated lives helped heal with metaphysical procedures.

It is truly a shameful lack of progression that there are barriers between the healers because of their various methods of healing. It limits healing progression as greatly as the barriers between the so-called overstructured religions which limit soul progression.

All healers *must* realize the limitless power and healing energies which can be harnessed by accepting each others' healing talents as a step in treating various mental and physical illnesses and injuries. There are various special needs for various special hurts.

Dieticians, holistic pharmacists, druggists, masseurs, chiropractors, osteopaths, dentists, opticians, medical doctors, surgeons, psychiatrists, psychologists, hypnotists, metaphysicians, and others all have their rightful place in healing the various ill and injured souls of low and high progression. For your own sake, realize that none of you healers are an island and through your inter-healing-action you *can cure all mental and physical illness and injury! Do not be stiff necked*, for if Creative Love acted as limited as you, creation would never have come into being!

All of you healers upon Earth-Eden pray and ask for guidance, then meditate and listen to the answers daily *for each of your individual patients*. All of you patients, pray and ask for guidance, then meditate and listen to the answers daily *for each of your individual healers*.

In meditation it is wise for both the healer and the patient to try to remember healing experiences of past incarnations such as in the healing temples of ancient Egypt and Atlantis. Then try to understand what Karma may be worked out through this situation and what lessons can be learned for the progression of your souls.

Last but most certainly not least, give heartfelt thanks, patient to healer, healer to patient, and all of you to Infinite, Intelligent, Creative Love in thought, word and deed for the healing, for the lessons learned, for the opportunity to serve as a channeling instrument of healing, and for becoming more perfect as Infinite, Intelligent, Creative Love is Perfect.

Infinite, Intelligent, Creative, Healing Love is *constantly* being channeled from Infinite, Intelligent, Creative Love to souls of all entities upon Earth-Eden with whom you in turn can demonstrate healing. If you do not feel you have progressed enough to heal yourself ask others to silently meditate for and with you in order to gain the understanding of the *truth* that you *can* heal yourself and others through your co-creative powers which the Pathshower demonstrated. The book of Job emphatically states: "Acquaint yourself now with the Almighty Creator and be at peace; there (through that peace) my (Creative Love's) good *shall* come to you. If you *return* to the Almighty Creator's ways, you *shall* build up (progress). Make your prayers to the Almighty Creator and the Almighty Creator shall hear you. When you decree something, it *shall* be established to you, and enlightenment *shall* shine upon your ways." (Job 22:21, 23, 27, 28)) Decree, demand, use your birthright gifts and you *shall* progress in the ability to heal yourself and others, spiritually and physically!

Love is the key factor to the highest degree of metaphysical healing. The metaphysical healing can only be as great as the progression of the healer; in other words, the healer heals in proportion to the healer's progression, no more, no less.

The metaphysician should always keep in mind the progressive thoughts of both patient and healer in order to help overcome not only sickness, but its root (regressive Karma), then eventually progress into health through Grace.

"(Infinite, Intelligent, Creative Love) is a very present help in time of trouble" (Ps. 46:1) and will *never* let you down, but will *constantly* help you to heal yourself and others if you but open up to Creative Consciousness as did the Pathshower. Realize your immortal power to heal mortal wounds and mortal sickness caused by mortal regression. The power found in Creative Consciousness can bring to *all* souls in the flesh upon Earth-Eden healing as well as enlightenment.

Chapter 28
Enlightenment Progression

Let us repeat what we have said in the preface of this book: "Everyone of your days is numbered right up to your last breath! Predestination? Yes and no. A contradiction? No. A paradox? Yes. Every soul has made a commitment before having entered upon Earth-Eden in each reincarnation." This was done in order to accomplish various soul progressions; however, each of you (souls in the flesh presently upon Earth-Eden) has been given free will to progress by your own doings with constant opportunity from Infinite, Intelligent, Creative Love to accomplish your tasks. What you do with this, your very precious allotted time, is entirely up to you!

What have you chosen so far? Light or darkness? Kindness or selfishness? Just as Infinite Intelligence knows the number of hairs on your head, so does Infinite Intelligence know what lies in your heart (Matt. 10:30)! Today is great with personal salvation, for it lies within *your* hands. Waste not another precious day, waste not another precious breath. Follow the path of the Master Pathshower in doing Love's Will and eventually returning *home* from where you strayed, and where you belong.

Each of you must demonstrate Creative Consciousness, the Light of the True Teachings of Creative Love. Take that Light with you wherever you go upon Earth-Eden or to the dimly lit areas of other realms which you may visit while in an out-of-the-body experience during sleep. Teach those souls so that they may learn the Truth and then they too shall shine forth in enlightenment of Creative Love. Teach that *not one soul* is any less loved by Creative Love at any one time, since they are *all* created equal in value, they are always *all* loved equally.

Teach others not to let the prejudices of lowly souls prevent them from progression. Bring enlightenment to those in need and they *will* be enlightened. Enlighten this realm and other realms by one soul at a time. Like little candles, being lit one at a time until there is great light, for light reflects light; therefore, there can be great soul progression. Love and take the risk of bringing Light and Love to those in need; the rewards are great indeed beyond your present comprehension. Strive for the day when bigotry and selfishness no longer enslave human thoughts. May this be the eternal millennium of revelation with a change for the better.

Creative Conscious enlightenment can bring Earth-Eden to the Paradise of Love's Perfection, rather than the doom of the end of the world (as you presently know it) of which the last book of the New Testament warns. It lies in *your hands*. It lies not in the power of the animals, the birds, the fishes nor the insects; it lies not in the power of the vegetation, the fungus cells nor the minerals. *It lies in the hands of human souls who have entered the flesh because of their own free will.* When will you begin to desire self less and Creative Love's Ways more? It is *not* too late, but soon it may be!

Do not be foolish and think that one person has no power. Do not waste precious time, for as each of you is as a grain of sand passing through the hourglass of destination, so each of you when united with others has power beyond measure. You *can* change Earth-Eden for the better. *You must!* In this matter you have little choice (because you have brought this upon yourselves). *Do not* say it was caused by others years before you were born, for you know that you have reincarnated *many* times upon Earth-Eden and each of you has either aided or not aided the present conditions. You *are* your friend's *and* your enemy's keeper (Gen. 4:9). Be enlightened to that fact!! Be enlightened as was the Pathshower. Be enlightened through the only avenue of enlightenment, Love; for Love is the foundation upon which all creation is established.

The Love of Infinite Intelligence is boundless, unending, ever growing and constant. It is the All in all of which everything is created. It is the All in all of which you and every soul are created. It is the All in all in which everything can progress to its fullest capacity. Love, that great virtue of human hope, is the reflection of

Infinite, Intelligent, Creative Love to *everyone*, which is Earth-Eden's constant hope. We emphatically, desperately hope for that love of each human who is presently incarnated in a vessel of flesh upon Earth-Eden today to be expressed through your free will toward each other and all other species.

You need not have as much fear of being invaded by creatures of other planets as you should have *dire fear* of the lack of love in each of your own hearts. What are you doing to help progress your planet physically and spiritually? You are *not doing enough*! Feed the hungry both physically and spiritually. Educate the unlearned both spiritually and literally. Protect the species which are in danger. Stop creating more dangerous mixtures of deadly chemicals which will poison the epidermis (soil) of Earth-Eden, for it will surely seep down into your water level from which no thirst will be quenched or from which no cleansing will be accomplished. Do you not care about those who come after you? Is your greed or your ignorance so great? Remember, "What *you sow, you* will reap" (Gal. 6:7). *What you do not prevent, you will experience* through the law of Karma (cause and effect) either in this life or *when you reincarnate*! If you care little about others could we at least interest, shame or frighten you into caring about your self?!

Be warned, you upon Earth-Eden, enlighten yourselves, for you need not fear alien creatures from other planets as much as the possible impending disaster of your own works of commission and omission. Infinite Intelligence "*Will not be mocked*" (Gal. 6:7)!

This message of alert has been given to rulers of nations and to rulers of religions many times in the last fifty years. Some have heeded, some have not. We are but one group of many who now, through channeling, are attempting to reach the multitudes through ordinary yet faithful, concerned souls such as our channeling instrument and your mentor Curt. Our task is to awaken Creative Consciousness in as many seekers as possible. You may ask what you can do. *You are a creation of Creative Love.* There is *much* you can do to enlighten *all* to do Love's Will. Let us give you some simple yet powerful ways in which you can be an instrument of Love, an instrument of Peace, an instrument of Enlightenment to bring about

Infinite, Intelligent, Loving Progression.

Understand that Infinite Intelligence has no competition. There is *no* devil who has any power over you. There are evil people, but each person is responsible for his or her own actions. It is individual greed and lack of compassion for others which creates hellish situations. Equally so, each of you through your gift of free will and your gift of co-creation from Creative Love has the ability to do the opposite of evil and that is the Will of Infinite Intelligence. This is *the* path well worth treading.

Understand your place in creation as a soul created by a Creative Love. Have hope in your fellow human beings for a progressive future upon Earth-Eden and radiate the love in which you are all created,the love which each of you can give to one another in times of joy and sorrow. The love of Infinite Intelligence constantly guides you, forgives you, protects you and always provides opportunities with which to progress to become one with each other, to become one with all creation, to become one with Creative Love and to return home in perfection. This is *the* path well worth treading.

Understand that Creative Consciousness was the way of thinking which the mind of the Teacher of teachers used. It is simply progressive thinking with Trust in Infinite Intelligence. It is all too easy to sit back and let the world pass you by. Progressive thinking tries again and again after it has failed to produce its progressive good the first, second or third time. Progressive thinking turns the non-progressive energy of doubting onlookers into personal progression. Personal progression turns into soul progression and in turn reflects upon other more progressive ideas, thus giving a greater span of more areas in which to progress with much more positiveness. Positiveness is the drive of Creative Consciousness and the knowledge that you are a creation of Creative Love is the source of that drive. Thus the use of Creative Consciousness makes you an instrument of peace, an instrument of enlightenment and an instrument of Infinite Intelligence! This is *the* path well worth treading.

Understand that each human entity upon Earth-Eden is a soul. *A living soul!* The flesh vessel which you inhabit, as better understood, is that which physically surrounds you, comes in various sizes, shapes and colors. There is *no* superiority as to size, shape or color. *None* is any better than another according to the flesh vessel, but there is *great* superiority among some living souls which inhabit the physical bodies. There is superiority in personal progression, soul progression and in the understanding of Creative Consciousness. The eons of bigotry which have clouded the progression of souls throughout recorded history and have hung above the path of enlightenment, darkening the view of many souls, and misleading them from Grace to a difficult Karma can be eliminated. You are all created in Love's likeness for all eternity, with the ability of free will, the ability to co-create and the ability to live according to Infinite Intelligence, thus eventually becoming at one with Infinite Intelligence. By simply *remembering* this fact you will begin to become an instrument of Love's peace. This is *the* path well worth treading.

Understand that there are limitless ways, situations, opportunities and vehicles with which each of you can become more and more the instruments of Love's Peace, Love's Enlightenment. As each living soul is an idea-seed of Infinite Intelligence which has the ability to co-create billions of idea-seeds of its own, it also has the free will to reflect Love's virtue in each of its idea-seeds such as kindness, compassion, honesty, justice, respect, and equality. Each idea-seed can be brought to its fruition of peace and enlightenment for the originator as well as the cosmos into which the idea-seeds can blossom. This is *the* path well worth treading.

> Understand that your soul is immortal, that it is created by Eternal, Peaceful, Creative Love and therefore you can reflect that loving peacefulness. As unrest brings you more unrest, so peacefulness brings you more peacefulness. Light reflects light, love reflects love, peace reflects peace, therefore you can reflect Infinite, Intelligence thus becoming an instrument of peaceful enlightenment. This is *the* path well worth treading.

As peace brings enlightenment, so does enlightenment of your origin bring peace. Your origin of being created by Infinite Intelligence establishes your at-one-ment with Infinite Intelligence from which you have strayed. That established at-one-ment origin can *never* be undone, lost or broken. You may have forgotten it, but Infinite Intelligence has not, and that is the reason books such as this are permitted to be written. We are but one small group of many groups who are presently attempting through instruments of enlightenment and peace, such as our instrument Curt through whom we are channeling upon Earth-Eden, to bring humanity (the last one-hundredth sheep) back into the fold of the peaceful, enlightened, progressive souls of Creative Love. "Hear O Israel (all entities upon Earth-Eden) the Lord thy God (Infinite, Intelligent, Creative Love), the Lord is One (you are all one in Infinite, Intelligent, Creative Love; therefore, strive to become one with each other, since you are *all* created with *equal* Love)" (Deut. 6:5).

"Your help (strength) comes from the Lord (Infinite

Intelligence), which made heaven and Earth-Eden (Creative Love of the seen and unseen, of the cosmos, and *you*)" (Ps. 121:2); therefore gain strength in the Love of that enlightenment and help your sisters and brothers in the flesh to go and do likewise, for such is the Kingdom of Heaven, for such is your inalienable right.

Some overstructured religions are not doing their utmost to bring about enlightenment. Too often they act in words only. To be clergy does not mean to be ordained only through ritual of an over-structured religion. To be clergy means for men and women to be ordained also through the thoughts, words and deeds of doing Love's Will, thus becoming ministers of kindness, compassion, honesty, justice, respect, and equality. Therefore *all* are called to the true clergy of living, loving souls by Living, Loving, Infinite Intelligence.

Rely upon your *devout* love for Infinite Intelligence. Put aside all needless fears of your future and fears for those whom you love. For as we have told you before, fear is nothing more or less than lack of trust in Infinite Intelligence. *All* will be given constant opportunity for progression both physically and spiritually according to the degree of each soul's present enlightenment; for does Infinite Intelligence not do the same for "the lilies of the field who neither spin nor toil? (Who do not manufacture or co-create)" (Matt. 6:28).

"Co-create" is not to be misunderstood as to mean "reproduce," for all of the various species have some type of ability to reproduce but only humans have the true ability to reflect Creative Love in a type of co-creation. Humans can co-create in astounding ways. They can foster specific strains of vegetation and animal lineage. They can co-create beauty in the arts and sciences. They can co-create in kindness, compassion, honesty, justice, respect, and equality to the *same* degree as Creative Love!! The Master stated "Greater works than I can you do" (John 14:12), and so it truly is if you but take advantage of the opportunities of this reflective progression which Infinite Intelligence constantly gives to you.

The New Testament states: "This then is the message which we have heard of him (Jesus) and declare unto you that God (Infinite, Intelligent, Creative Love) is light (enlightenment), and in him

(Infinite, Intelligent, Creative Love) is no darkness (iniquity) at all." (1 John 1:5)

In the physical, light can be brought to shine through darkness to cut a visible path; so too in the spiritual, for enlightenment can be brought to shine through iniquity to cut a progressive path. This process can *never* be reversed in either the physical or spiritual, in that darkness *cannot* be brought to shine through light and that iniquity *cannot* be brought to shine through enlightenment. *It is a one-way path—progressive!!* The darkness or lack of enlightenment falls away into the *nothingness* which it is when the light of Creative Consciousness is allowed by an individual to penetrate its soul. The same result is possible for families, groups of individuals and nations. There is no limitation to numbers. This is the consistency of Creative Love's free will given to each of you, which is ever-present now and even after the change called death.

Once you secure Creative Consciousness as your anchor of salvation, of stability, of trust, you will learn that you are firmly anchored in the foundational Truths of Infinite, Intelligent, Creative Love, and have sustainment of strength so that waves of ignorance and greed are of no threat to you.

Understand that it is Everlasting Love from which you came and it is Everlasting Love to which you must return. From Everlasting Love to Everlasting Love without end, *this is highest enlightenment*! Know that Infinite, Intelligent, Creative Love not only limitlessly cared about you before you entered the flesh, and not only limitlessly will care about you after you have left the flesh, but does indeed *limitlessly care about you now while you are in the flesh!!! Therefore realize that you are surrounded by Everlasting Love now, this very moment, and never—not even for one split second—does it ever leave you!!!!*

This enlightenment can shed great understanding on many Bible truths such as: "I can do all things (progressions) through him (Creative Consciousness) which strengthens (enlightens) me." (Phil. 4:13). "The Lord (Infinite, Intelligent, Creative Love) is my light (enlightenment) and my salvation (my return to righteous ways); whom (what) shall I fear? The Lord (Infinite, Intelligent, Creative Love) is the strength of my life (the only source and constant supplier); of whom (of what) shall I be afraid" (Ps. 27:1).

Too often needless fear brings about needless anger. Anger is a poison to one's thoughts and can cause harmful regression to both the physical and the spiritual if permitted to do so. Anger can also be overcome by working with the aforementioned scripture verses in Philippians and the Psalms. After realizing the wasteful energy of fear and anger, stand back and witness the calming progression of Infinite, Intelligent, Creative Love as you demonstrate free will to its fullest extent in that of doing Love's Will. Think "Love-ward." Do not let today's thoughts be tethered to yesterday's limited knowledge, rather prepare in the present for future progression.

Understand Creative Conscious enlightenment as being individual as well as collective. Understand that it *can* be tapped, and that Love is its source, (Infinite Intelligence of the cosmos and all that exists both physical and spiritual). Understand *your* importance to yourself, the whole of creation and to Creative Love. Understand the importance of your existence, your thoughts, your words, and your deeds. Understand that Creative Love cares about *you* more than about all of the stars of the universe. Understand that in *all* of Love's existing creation a place is prepared for each of you in whatever realm you are, and a place is prepared for you in whatever realm you will go to according to your progressive deeds (John 14:2).

You progress in soul in proportion to your demonstration of Love's Will through kindness, compassion, honesty, justice, respect, and equality to *all*, which generates spiritual and physical energies with which to progress even higher.

You always have been "created" as Creative Love always has been "Created". If each of you entities upon Earth-Eden would but take the time to realize your existence and your co-creative abilities, you would create more progressive opportunities for yourself, and therefore your capacity for demonstrating Love's Will would increase.

The Pathshower demonstrated the highest form of enlightenment through Creative Consciousness. He became at-one with Infinite, Intelligent, Creative Love through demonstrating Creative

Consciousness to the fullest. As husbands and wives are made one, as friends are made one, as life-partners are made one, so can *all* souls become one with Creative Love as the Master taught and demonstrated to become at-one, to become perfect as Infinite Intelligence is perfect (Matt. 5:48).

Understand that God is Infinite, Intelligent, Loving, Creative Principle and that you are created in that same Principle. Use the Infinite within you. Use the Intelligence within you. Use the Creativeness within you. Use the Love within you, then by small yet constant steps ascend the staircase of Principle, thus becoming more perfect as Love is Perfect.

Understand that as Infinite Intelligence was your help in ages of past lives, so is Infinite Intelligence your help in this life and will be your help in lives to come; ever present, ever supplying you with *all* you need to progress. Awaken to this spiritual enlightenment.

It is by following the Principles of Infinite, Intelligent, Creative Love that you can prevent personal and collective "Armageddon" (Rev. 16:16), that you can prevent personal and collective spiritual and physical upheaval and destruction upon Earth-Eden.

It is by following the Principles of Infinite, Intelligent, Creative Love that you *can* bring personal and collective *order* out of chaos, that you can bring personal and collective light and enlightenment into darkness by good deeds which are known in Hebrew as mitzvahs.

Chapter 29
Mitzvah Progression

How often have you wished to be able to erase past non-progressive thoughts? How often have you wished to be able to take back non-progressive words? How often have you wished to be able to undo past non-progressive deeds? Those wishes, if sincere enough, may have the possibility of becoming reality. Although it may not be possible to undo the past in toto, you certainly can bridge the gap. A "mitzvah" is best described as a good deed and what else should you be doing upon Earth-Eden if not good deeds? To sum it up simply is to call a mitzvah the bridge between Karma (cause and effect) and Grace (at-one-ment with Infinite, Intelligent, Creative Love).

The Old Testament promises the rewards of principal mitzvahs when demonstrating kindness to your aged father (and mother) which will serve as a sin (regression) offering. In other words, a mitzvah is a good deed bridging the path from Karma to Grace.

In the ten commandments you are taught to "Honor your father and your mother, that your days may be long (that your life upon Earth-Eden may be long-filled with joy in reflecting Creative Love from you to your parents)" (Exod. 20:12). Often in a sense you can undo past ill thoughts, ill words and ill deeds by now showing your honor to family members and others in thought, word and deed through kindness, compassion, honesty, justice, respect and equality. It is simply a matter of Love-oriented attitude.

Chapter 30
Attitude Progression

Dearly beloved fellow-created souls, we wish to make this, our last chapter of Volume I, as personal and heart-provoking in Creative Consciousness as possible. We wish to iterate, to remind, to lovingly badger you to be aware constantly of your mental attitude towards life. We wish to give you a progressive declaration intended to help you promote foresight. The source of this blessed assurance is from the *only* source, Infinite, Intelligent, Creative Love.

Life is what you make or do not make of it, depending upon your attitude. Your future is in your hands; but your hands are not enough. You must place your hands in Creative Love's hands. Infinite Intelligence has given you free will and a mind which can give your soul constant progression if you but retain Creative Consciousness in your daily attitude. Be concerned about all the possibilities which lie upon your daily paths. Mind is ever the builder. As you did think, so you were; as you now think, so you are; as you will think, so you will be. If you think the thoughts of "not making it," "losing," or "being below par," do not expect to "make it," "win," or "be above par." Stop fooling yourself. Visualize your future spiritual achievements with the attitude that they will be yours.

Re-read Chapter 1, Personal Progression, and re-check your thoughts, words and deeds. Change your negative concepts. Replace all negative words which you have been using with positive words. Use the mini-concept changer cards. Be assured of your success which is your birthright as a soulful creation of Creative Love. You *are* not alone, you *never* were alone, you *never* will be alone. You can do *all* soul progressive things through Creative Consciousness which is constantly with you and which constantly strengthens you (Phil. 4:13).

When you have questions or doubts, turn to Infinite,

Intelligent, Creative Love for answers and help, *knowing* that the supply-cup is there and running over for your soul progression even before you realize the need (Ps. 23:5). Whenever a problem or query lies before you, always let your mind reflect Love's idea of you through Creative Consciousness as did the Pathshower. Think of all the positive probabilities, possibilities and constant opportunities which Creative Love makes ever available to you for your soul progression with which to enter Grace and return *home.*

Words such as "doubt" or "failure" are very limited, for they only exist or seem to exist in human thoughts. They *do not exist* in Creative Consciousness, they *do not exist* in Infinite Intelligence, therefore they are not real, not progressive, not truthful. They are a lie, or *nothing*. Infinite Intelligent thoughts are the opposite, for they *are* progressive, they *are* truthful, they are real, as *Infinite Intelligence is*!

Metaphysics can play an immense part in the progression with which to achieve proper attitudes towards all situations. The physical state is but a day in the life of eternity. The spiritual state is endless existence in the life of the soul. *Know* "from whence your help cometh" (Ps. 121:2). Foundational Truth is *knowing* that Infinite, Intelligent, Creative Love is a constant source of help, reliance, life, and love (Ps. 9:9). Believe and repent, progress and realize that you *have* the power within you to move mountains. Have a mountain-moving attitude and you *will* move mountains (Matt. 17:20). Realize that you *can* overcome sin (self); therefore, you *can* overcome sickness (not reflecting Love's image) and death (needing to reincarnate no more) once and forever.

Attitude can be expressed in two ways, namely *positude* or *negatude*. Change your attitude about yourself if it is not positude, change your attitude about others, for there are *no* strangers or immigrants in Creative Love's world. Get to know yourself better, get to know others better. Take the risk in making new friends, for they may be taking the same risk of getting to know you!! You are *all* Creative Love's children! When you need some encouragement, ask someone to help. Four hands work better than two; add Creative Love to that group and you *will* succeed! Do not be insensitive to your own needs and to the needs of others. Turn the insensitiveness into spiritual "in-cense" (inner sense)! Meditation and incense have much in common in that a little of each goes a long way; therefore, let your meditative life progress and rise as incense to heavenly, Love-Willed heights!

Your attitude either makes or breaks the moment, precious moments which will not return. Your attitude either makes or breaks the day, precious days which will not return. Your attitude either makes or breaks your present incarnation, a precious incarnation which will not return and is filled with the opportunities of experiencing and progressing in Creative Love's Beauty and Harmony. We acknowledge the difficulties which each one of you has in your daily physical existence, but we also know the resplendent reality of rising above each trying step which leads you away from Karma, towards Grace. Follow these our tenets, follow the still, small voice within you (1 Kings 19:12), and follow the "Light of the World" (John 8:12) which is the example of the Master Pathshower through the attitude of Creative Consciousness. Make your attitude hopeful, make your attitude positive, make your attitude trustful in Creative Love.

We soulfully urge you to look around and gear your attitude to notice the physical beauty of your environment. Open the aesthetic bud within your heart and the aptitude bud of achievement will blossom forth as well, thus elevating your spirit, thus progressing in soul. Then, after you have taken a good, long look at the natural beauty upon Earth-Eden, remember that, "Eye has not seen, ear has not heard, nor has it entered into the hearts and minds of many what Creative Love has waiting for those who love themselves, who love their friends, who love their enemies, thus who love Creative Love" (1 Cor. 2:9).

Look for Creative Love's beauty in everything you see no matter how much ugliness seems to surround it. Listen for Creative Love's harmony in everything you hear no matter how much discord seems to try to distort it. Extract Creative Love's compassion from all whom you meet no matter how cruel they may seem to be. Seek the good, seek the fine, seek the progressiveness in all with whom you come into daily contact. Change your negative concepts into the attitude of Creative Consciousness, and remember that it is by small yet constant steps that you ascend the staircase of soul progression, and that *Infinite, Intelligent, Creative Love is always present to guide you step by step even when you stumble.* We love you deeply and Creative Love loves you compassionately with the peace of understanding which, foolishly, all too many upon Earth-Eden feel is beyond their ability to practice (Phil. 4:7).

As Curt is our channeling instrument of peace, so Curt is Creative Love's channeling instrument of peace, though he stumbles as he progresses. As each of you has the ability to stumble, so each of you has the ability to progress, and so each has the ability to be a channeling instrument of peace. Where there is hatred, sow peace; where there is doubt, sow trust in Creative Love; where there is darkness of prejudice towards any other human being because of age, gender, sexual orientation, race or religion, sow the teachings of the Light (Enlightenment) of the World of equal sisterly and brotherly love; where there is greed (the root sin or self), sow the teachings of the Master Pathshower by doing unto others as you would have others do unto you (Matt. 7:12) lest you continue to struggle under Karma (cause and effect) rather than progress in soul by entering Grace through Creative Consciousness.

We still have not given you any names as to who we are, but at this point will tell you that we are Kielahn, the master soul of all past incarnations of Curt H. von Dornheim, and the Teaching Angels of Creative Consciousness, teaching the Infinite Presence within each of you, demonstrating kindness, compassion, honesty, justice, respect and equality resulting in peace. Now, do you believe anymore or any less of what we have been proclaiming with profound love to you? *For Creative Love's sake, listen to us when we tell you that Armageddon need not come to pass* (Rev. 16:16)! Rather, each soul can have a personal final battle of good conquering evil (self meeting self). "*Today* is your day of salvation" (2 Cor. 6:2). Through Creative Love's Ways, love one another even as Creative Love Loves you. Will you now progress any more or any less in your attitudes towards yourselves, each other, and Infinite, Intelligent, Creative Love since we have told you who we are? We *have* stumbled and we *have* progressed. We *have* stumbled less and we *have* progressed more. Believe that the Master Pathshower *is, was* and *will be* the example for you to follow. This is *not* impossible for you, rather it is your golden privilege which *must* become your goal! There is life after the change called death; there is justice in the courts of Infinite Intelligence! *God is Infinite, Intelligent, Creative Love, which always has, always does and always will love you so much as to permit you free will; use it progressively !!!*

Much anti-Creative Consciousness is presently upon Earth-Eden. "Creative Consciousness," "Christ Consciousness" and the "Creative Mind" are all the same. It is "*That* mind which was in the Teacher of teachers" (Phil. 2:5), that way of thinking, speaking and acting which is the Will of Creative Love as the Pathshower demonstrated and *it is to be followed*! Awake from your spiritual slumbering, oh you upon Earth-Eden, repent from your non-loving ways and begin to tread the path of righteousness (Eph. 5:14), eventually ascending Jacob's ladder (Gen. 28:10-13) by small yet constant steps with Creative Love for the progression of your precious souls bringing about peace upon Earth-Eden with goodwill to *all* (Luke 2:14). You have been given the free will and the ability to do so; however, if you selfishly do not tread the path of righteousness, what do you think will become of you personally after the change called death?

If many souls around you seem not to progress and seem to be on the road of perishing, let it be *you* who does *not* lose the progression of your soul! Let it be *you* who *progresses* in thought, word and deed through kindness, compassion, honesty, justice, respect, and equality towards yourself, friends, strangers and enemies! Let it be *you* who will clean up the planet Earth-Eden to make it free from litter, acid rain, poisonous chemicals in the soil and explosive nuclear destruction. Let it be *you* who demonstrates Creative Consciousness to bring about peace upon Earth-Eden! Let it be *you* who will need to go out no more (*reincarnate no more*) through Karma (cause and effect)! Let it be *you* who *will* return *home* through Grace (*Creative Love's way*) to Infinite, Intelligent, Creative Love. What good is it if you gain the material world for a few short years but lose the progression of your soul (Matt. 16:26)?!

If we did not love you with Creative Conscious Love, we would not have channeled the writings of this book through our dear colleague and your faithful mentor, Curt. Take what you understand, take what you need, take what you consider beneficial from these pages and progress in soul.

What you do not understand, what you think you do not need, what you do not consider beneficial, leave for the time being; but later, be it in a few weeks or in a few years, read these writings over again and progress in soul more and more in order to return *home*.

We will leave you with these Five Ponderings which we wish for you to silently ponder upon every day of your present incarnation.

Ponder upon the ways of becoming more aware of your feelings.

Ponder upon the ways of becoming wiser in your soul progression.

Ponder upon the ways of correcting relationships with others.

Ponder upon the ways of becoming at one with Creative Love.

Ponder upon the ways of helping others to do the same.

Remember, Infinite Intelligence is no respecter of age, gender, sexual orientation, race or religion (Acts 10:34). Infinite Intelligence is a respecter of hearts. What does your heart contain?

Be assured, you have the ability and power to progress through free will! Creative Love loves you and cares about each one of you individually, equally, beyond your present understanding! Come home! Follow the Pathshower as he demonstrated Creative Consciousness, which this book explains as a guide, helping to map the path of becoming a mentor of foresight!

Your angel teachers from the Third Realm
who are only presently beyond you.

From Your Channeling Author

Dear Reader:

I wish to say just a few closing words. Whatever your feelings may be, remember that Infinite, Intelligent, Creative Love is closer to us than our own breath and, through free will, tries us in a furnace of love to have the dross of selfishness cast off so that each of us may become goldenly perfect in soul (Wisdom 3:5-6) even as Creative Love is perfect (Matt. 5:48), thus making straight the path which leads home, since Earth-Eden is not our goal. I pray daily for all of our souls to progress and wish for our eventual return home. I shall gladly continue to channel through our loving, caring angel teachers whose source is the Only Source (Infinite, Intelligent, Creative Love)!

Although our angel teachers are not known to me by name, they certainly have made themselves known to me by their various personalities. They have become as loving friends, teachers and mentors. It is indeed a privilege for me to feel their presence each time I sit down to write.

As teacher of Creative Consciousness I serve best, hopefully, to guide and encourage through channeling for students of Creative Consciousness, to help you learn and practice its lessons of enlightenment dealing with reincarnation, and soul-progression which have been written for all seeking souls of this planet.

Creative Consciousness is a soul-progressive path bringing peace and enlightenment to all entities upon Earth-Eden, now and even after the change called death, through the thirty progressions of this channeled metaphysical textbook.

The study of Creative Consciousness will constantly reward you with spiritual understanding of Infinite, Intelligent, Creative Love upon the level to which you have progressed, and will constantly elevate your soul progression as you continue to progress through sincere study and demonstration.

I hope to instill in you the motive to energize progression of peace on earth in the good will of caring for friend or stranger, and to alarm you of the dire necessity to begin seriously to cleanse the air, water, soil and spirit of Earth-Eden.

Finally, I hope lovingly to inspire the awakening of confidence within you and to remind you of Creative Love's Love for us all.

These are the tasks which I, as a channeling mentor, strive to fulfill, and invite you to do likewise with benevolence and love.

Let us not be strangers. If you have had any experiences pertaining to angels, please contact me, and if possible I would like to compile a book to share those experiences with others which is to be titled "Angels on Call." I also would like to receive any questions you may have concerning Creative Consciousness; and if possible, I may complile a book with the channeled answers which is to be titled "Angel Answers to Your Questions."

Let us each strive in Creative Consciousness for soul progression for ourselves and for each other since we walk not alone.

Caringly,

Curt H. von Dornheim

Your channeling author
who is only temporarily upon Earth-Eden

Creative Consciousness Vol 1

by Curt H von Dornheim

A guide to recognizing your spirituality and putting your ultimate belief in Infinite Love in practice in your daily life. Through implementing the practice of Creative Consciousness you will bring direction, peace, love and effectiveness to your life and in your actions towards others. This channeled text leads you step by step, gently yet firmly, towards an understanding of the inviolate connection between mind and body, Earth and the spirit realms. Creative Consciousness does not replace religion, but helps you to make those teachings active with a greater understanding of yourself and your soul.

6 x 9, softbound, 240 pages,
ISBN 0-89404-220-3 $16.95

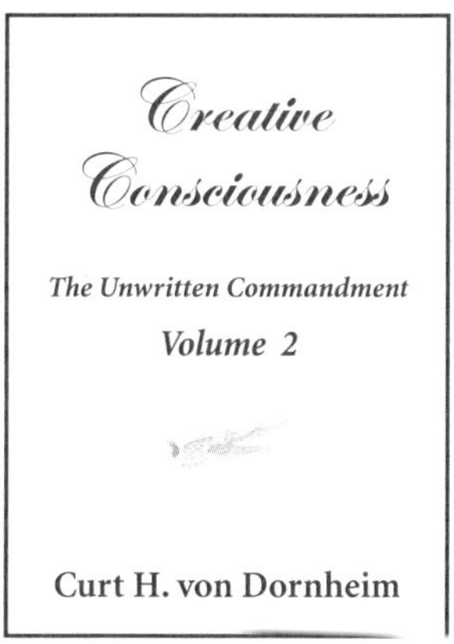

Creative Consciousness Vol 2

by Curt H von Dornheim

The second in a series to help you recognize your spirituality and bring your ultimate belief in Infinite Love into your daily actions. In implementing the practice of Creative Consciousness towards specific aspects of your life, this channeled text leads you gently yet firmly towards a greater understanding of the connection between mind and body, Earth and the spirit realms. Creative Consciousness does not replace religion, but helps you towards a greater understanding of yourself and your soul, and how your beliefs and actions affect others now and in the future, as well as having a bearing on the hereafter.

6x9, softbound, 160 pages, Aug. 1997
ISBN 0-89404-221-1 $16.95

Creative Consciousness Vol. 1
Seeker's Study Guide, Chapters 1-30

by Curt H von Dornheim

A companion to Creative Consciousness Vol. I, the Seeker's Study Guide is a continuation of study of the textbook. The Study Guide is like having a friendly mentor at your side,helping you understand and progress. There are ten questions and a 'task' question for each chapter, to help you focus on the lessons of progression in that chapter. Space is provided to write the answer under each question. It is recommended that the textbook, Creative Consciousness Vol. I, be open for reference when needed.

8-1/2 x 11, softbound, Aug. 1997
ISBN 0-89404-226-2 $12.95

Creative Consciousness Vol. 2
Seeker's Study Guide, Chapters 31-60

by Curt H. von Dornheim

A companion to Creative Consciousness Vol. II, the Seeker's Study Guide is a continuation of study of the textbook. This Study Guide follows the same format as the one for Creative Consciousness Vol. I with ten questions and a 'task' question for each chapter, to help you focus on the lessons of progression in that chapter. Space is provided to write the answer under each question. It is recommended that the textbook, Creative Consciousness Vol. II, be open for reference when needed.

8-1/2 x 11, softbound, Aug. 1997
ISBN 0-89404-227-0 $12.95

The official metaphysical textbooks, Creative Consciousness Volume 1 and Volume 2, plus Course Exams towards an academic teaching certificate, or an academic student certificate, are available for the forming of independent study groups. See page 238 for address and phone numbers.

The Little Baron's Christmas Angel

by Curt H von Dornheim

As the Little Baron faces Christmas without his parents, a Christmas Angel appears to comfort him. At first he thinks it was only a dream, but in more visitations the angel helps him through the loss of Grandfather Baron, and his manor house. The angel gives him confidence for the future which ultimately reaffirms the angel's reality and the credibility of the angel's beautiful messages.

A timeless tale of turning stumbling blocks into stepping stones for the Little Baron, his old orange cat Mr. Tobles and his loving family. The Christmas Angel shows how to accept the inevitable changes of live and how to recognize what is truly important.

The Little Baron's Christmas Angel is not channeled, but is a Creative Consciousness story of "myth and memory." A perfect gift.

9x7, hardbound, 64 pages, Sept. 1997
ISBN 0-89404-222-X $12.95

Angel Messages

by Curt H von Dornheim

Angel Messages offers a positive perspective to the frustrations and anxieties of everyday life. In messages from two lines to two pages, these writings lift the burden of problems and perplexities through helpful, thought-provoking and sometimes humorous presentations of human life while reminding you that you are never alone.

9x7, hardbound, 96 pages, Oct. 1997
ISBN 0-89404-223-8 $14.95

Visiting with the Angels

by Curt H von Dornheim

"From my earliest years, I have been able to see angels and receive mes-

sages from them, though I learned early not to tell just anyone about these visits." And so begins the unfolding of the story of the rather unusual life of Curt H. von Dornheim. He started writing down these messages at the age of ten. Psychic and clairvoyant, he knew things that were going to happen or had happened. His friends thought he was "strange." In the pursuit of understanding this unusual "gift," by the time he was in his teens he had read the Bible, the sacred writings of other religions, parapsychological and metaphysical writings. Curt had the psychic ability, but not control of it—it wasn't something he could turn on or off at will. He tried cabinet work, and seances, joined a group of would-be clairvoyants. While in the Army, he was a chaplain's assistant and organist. He went on to become a professional church organist, retiring from this two years ago to devote full time to the teaching of Creative Consciousness. Over these past fifteen years he has taught Creative Consciousness to numerous classes along the East Coast.

Visiting with the Angels has been written at the request of many of his students to tell the story of how the wonderful teachings all came into being. As he was writing, much more was channeled, making this a truly remarkable book.

6x9, softbound, 192 pages Sept. 1997
ISBN 0-89404-224-6 $16.95

The Children's Angel Clock

by Curt H von Dornheim

Sixteen-year old Hope finds a dusty old clock with no hands one day as she rummages in the corners of her Aunt Joy's little antique shop. On the face is a lovely picture of angels. Intrigued, they clean it and search for the hands, and a key to fit the hole in the back so they can wind it. But this is not as simple as it sounds, and so begins the mystery of The Children's Angel Clock. This delightful surprising story is, in the author's words, "for grownups to read to children thus permitting the grownups to enjoy, remember and learn from as well."

9x7, hardbound, 128 pages, 1998
ISBN 0-89404-225-4 $16.95

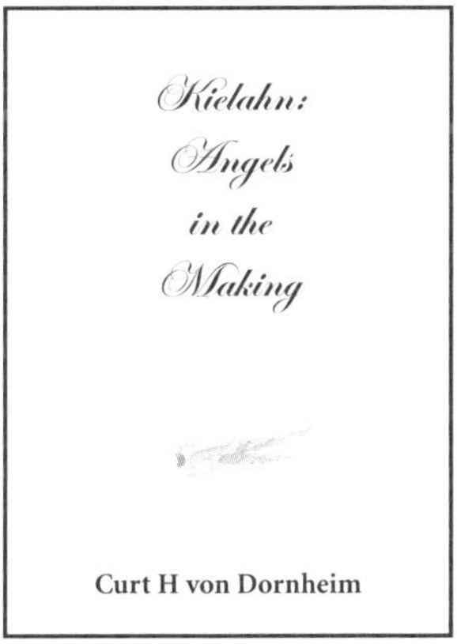

Kielahn: Angels in the Making

by Curt H von Dornheim

Lessons in love are at the heart of this book. Whatever your daily life requires of you can be accomplished in a loving way. As God is Infinite, Intelligent, Creative Love, so you are a being of love. However, too often, we humans let temporary worries and perceived obligations get in the way. *Angels in the Making* lovingly walks you along the path to see the light of love and learn to open yourself, allowing love to flow freely and be received in return. As you progress in love—agape—the everlasting spiritual love for friends and family, you grow spiritually, enabling yourself to live life on earth more fully, happily, and satisfied. Make every action you take be one of love. As you think more angelic thoughts, you speak more angelic words, you demonstrate more angelic deeds, you progress to the making of an angel. Why? Because such are the qualities and virtues which are found upon higher spiritual realms. Each step along the path of love is a step in that of an 'angel in the making'...you...as you progress towards your ultimate destiny of at-one-ment. This metaphysical text has been lovingly channeled by Kielahn, an angel in the making.

6x9, 128 pages, softbound, Oct. 1997
ISBN 0-89404-228-9 $14.95

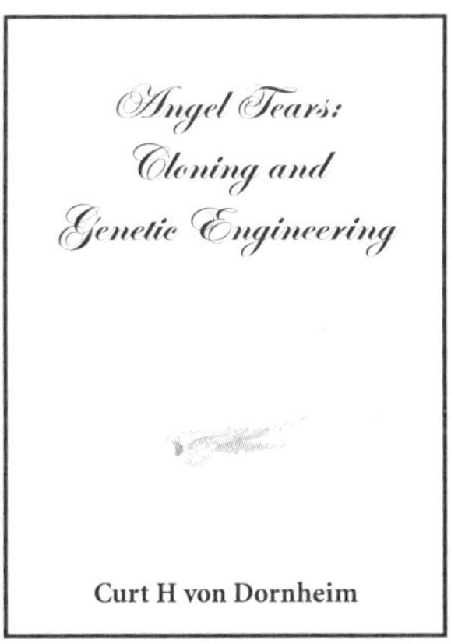

Angel Tears: Cloning and Genetic Engineering

by Curt H von Dornheim

You can feel the anguish of the angels throughout this thought-provoking book. So you've cloned a sheep! But with all your God-given free will and co-creative abilities, you still can not co-create well enough to permit human cloning. If a human were cloned, would the clone be human? Would it have a soul? Would it be granted human rights? Would it be kept in a cage, a source of spare parts when needed? Could it reproduce? Would anyone love it? Co-creative abilities must be used for loving progress, not for scientific ego. Genetic engineering and cloning go together as scientific breakthroughs that must be very carefully monitored under strict legal, moral and ethical parameters. Have you thought about the possibilities? Some genetic engineering offers much improvement in relief of needless suffering, but are we approaching the point where if something cannot be cured in the womb, the fetus will suffer forced abortion because it will be a social pariah or financial burden—regardless of the parents desires?

This timely channelled metaphysical text should be read by everyone, before our world becomes something far worse than the most horrific sci-fi story writers can conceive.

6 x9, 96 pages, softbound, July 1997
ISBN 0-89404-230-0 $12.95

Angels to the Rescue

by Curt H von Dornheim

Dr Tyler Thornton isn't burned out, he's burned up! He's worked the ER for years. Until recently, he felt his work was valuable, particularly for the elderly. But now more and more of his patients are kids. O'd on drugs, shot in a gang war…just kids…very dead kids. Tyler decides to take a sabbatical. He believes he can do a lot more if he gets out in the field and reaches them before they hit the ER. But first he has to convince his board of directors to give him time off.

You see, Dr Tyler Thornton's ER isn't of this Earth, it's on the second realm; the emergency clinic of ontological psychology, and his board of directors is five fellow angels headed by one archangel. They grant his request and give him the ability to take whatever form—or become invisible—as suits his purpose, though he is required to check in regularly.

Thornton's first target is Billy Joe Barker, a televangelist who has gotten wealthy preaching fear, but has dark secrets of his own. At a prayer meeting, Billy Joe asks for volunteers to man his newest venture, a radio show called Angels to the Rescue, where people with problems can call for help. Thornton is the first volunteer, and proves to be *very* good at it. His landlady, Jewish medium Sarah Krakow, quickly becomes the middle-aged black doctor's willing accomplice in this fast-paced metaphysical novel.

6 x 9, 292 pages, softbound, 1998
ISBN 0-89404-229-7 $18.95

The Creative Consciousness line of books described on pages 231-237 are available through book, angel, metaphysical and new age outlets, or direct from the publisher. Publication dates and prices are subject to change; please check availability before ordering. Individuals ordering by mail, please add $5.00 shipping and handling per order.

The official metaphysical textbooks, Creative Consciousness Volume 1 and Volume 2, plus Course Exams towards an academic teaching certificate, or an academic student certificate, are available for the forming of independent study groups.

For details, please write or E-mail to:

Creative Consciousness
Dept. of Academics
c/o AZTEX Corporation
P.O. Box 50046
Tucson, AZ 85703-1046

Voice 520-882-4656
Fax 520-792-8501

E-mail: ac@aztexcorp.com

Additional information may also be found on our web page:
http://www.aztexcorp.com

Registration Form

I am interested in learning more about the teachings of Creative Consciousness, and being notified of new publications, classes or seminars that may be forthcoming. Please put me on your mailing list.

Name ____

Address ____

City ______________________ State ____ Zip __________

E-mail ____

Phone ____

If you have a preferred bookstore or other retail establishment where you do business, and would like us to keep them informed as to new titles, etc., please list the store's address below.

Store name _______________________________________

Attn: ____

Address ____

City ______________________ State ____ Zip __________

E-mail ____

Phone ____

Note: It is suggested you make a copy of this form and send it to us, leaving the original in the book to identify it as yours. Please mail completed registration forms to: Creative Consciousness, Dept. R., P. O. Box 50046, Tucson, AZ 85703-1046

Agape